The Lost Art of Doing
NOTHING

Originally published in the U.S. in 2021 by The Experiment, LLC.
This edition published by arrangement with The Experiment, LLC.

First Indian Edition,
Published in 2024 by:
Embassy Book Distributors
120, Great Western Building, Maharashtra Chamber of
Commerce Lane, Fort, Mumbai 400 023, India
Tel: (+9122) -30967415, 22819546
Email: info@embassybooks.in
www.embassybooks.in

ISBN: 978-81-19726-99-8

Distribution Centres:
Mumbai, Ahmedabad, Bangalore, Kolkata, Chennai, Hyderabad,
New Delhi, Pune

Printed & bound in India by Thomson Press India Ltd.

The Lost Art of Doing NOTHING

How the Dutch Unwind with NIKSEN

MAARTJE WILLEMS & LONA AALDERS

Translated by Laura Vroomen

EMBASSY BOOKS
www.embassybooks.in

* Dutch comedian and writer

CONTENTS

TOPICS

- **What is *niksen*?**
- **Why is it so hard?**
- **How to teach yourself**

PREFACE

Welcome to *The Lost Art of Doing Nothing*—also known as *niksen*. Niksen is not just any old art; it's a higher art. It's almost impossible to do nothing at all. To show you just how hard it is—and also to show you we have some street cred—we open with a quote by Blaise Pascal, a seventeenth-century French influencer. Hardly anybody is good at doing nothing, and no one can keep it up for long. Before you know it, existential questions start bubbling up that spell the end of any aimless chilling. Because the answers are probably not forthcoming, you start looking for distraction again, something to fill the time.

> Nothing is so insufferable to man as to be completely at rest. . . . He then feels his nothingness.
>
> —Blaise Pascal, *Pensées*

If not these important life questions, then your growling stomach sends you scuttling to the fridge. Suddenly you find yourself preparing a snack instead of doing nothing.

Our whole lives, Lona (who did the illustrations) and I (Maartje) have been trying to come to grips with the hustle and bustle of modern life. We listened to Oprah, who told us to live our "best life," which is easier said than done. It implies that there is a menu, such that with hindsight you can be accused of not making the best choices. You have only yourself to blame for the fact that it hasn't all been Instagrammable. Nobody sets out to mess up, or to live their worst life. We're all searching for ways to become better people, cope with setbacks, and fight the demons in ourselves and our past. For centuries, we've been sharing our tips and tricks to do just that—including, these days, neat winning formulas: Twenty steps to happiness! Ten reasons to embrace your imperfections! On the face of it these popular lists are clear and attainable, but in reality they only add to your already overcrowded schedule. You're supposed to emerge stronger from a breakup, learn more effectively, relax more, create more me-time, exercise, eat well, do community service, have a meaningful job, start a family, and on and on. This is why Lona has been teetering on the edge of burnout since kindergarten and why I have to conquer my towering fear of failure day in and day out.

We have searched for ways to calm our churning minds and to master our sad feelings by trying all kinds of things: therapy (heartily recommended), as well as sensory deprivation therapy, meditation, yoga, Pilates, hiking in the woods, vacationing in winter, cuddling rabbits, horse riding, and crafting. Lifestyle trends come and go, and they all tell us what to do. An app like Headspace, full of wonderful meditations, promises to make us happy and healthy. We're urged to live our dream life. It's maddening!

It turns out that all these years, amid this jumble of goals, the Dutch have been sitting on the solution: niksen, the art of doing nothing. It made the news around the world, which in turn made the headlines in the Netherlands. But the confusion around the subject was palpable. The Dutch looked to one another for support, trying to get their heads around it. "Do you know what this is about?" they sheepishly asked, not wanting to be found out and seem stupid. Nope, nobody had any idea. Sure, some offices had "quiet rooms," but they were mostly used for breastfeeding or for getting changed ahead of the office party. And we remember only too well when, lying in the grass among the fresh daisies, we were told off for being "a lazy so-and-so" and urged to "stop niksen, right this minute." It wasn't exactly nice to be accused of doing nothing.

WHAT IS IT?

So what exactly is niksen? It's not easy to put a finger on it, precisely because there's so little to it. Niksen is the absence of any other activity. The Dutch dictionary defines *niks* as a variation of *niets*, meaning "nothing," so the verb *niksen* means "to do nothing." It has distinct overtones of disapproval. As in, "Look at that one, sitting on his ass all day, not getting anything done." It doesn't sound as meditative as we'd like. Then there's the associated *niksnut*, or "good-for-nothing," another negative term. Someone who doesn't do anything useful, who doesn't contribute anything to society, is a niksnut.

The word *niks* probably came from eighteenth-century High German *nicks* or *nix*, variants of *nichts*. It was most likely introduced in the Netherlands by soldiers—or so we read in an etymological dictionary published in the early twentieth century that we consulted at the Meertens Institute in Amsterdam, a research organization that focuses on diversity in Dutch language and culture.

Idling never helped put out a fire.

It's not known who came up with the luminous idea of turning *niks* into a verb. The Dutch have a knack for taking nouns and making them into verbs. An obvious example is *wijn* and *wijnen*, "wine" and "wining"—not necessarily in combination with dining (more on that soon). We also like *schemeren*, from *schemer*, meaning "dusk," referring to that time around sunset, when it's getting just dark enough to switch on some lamps or light a few candles, and you're feeling all cozy on the couch, savoring the last golden light of the day. And then there's *tafelen* (dining), or even better, *natafelen*! Combining *after* and *table*, it refers to that

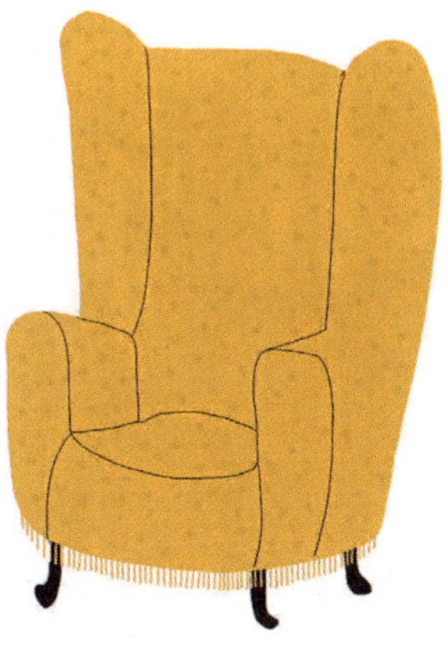

We are here on Earth to FART AROUND and don't let ANYBODY tell you differen

KURT VONNEGUT

leisurely time post-dinner when you and your fellow diners are busy setting the world to rights. If *natafelen* caught on it would be one hell of a trend, and the Dutch would be its world leaders! We'd no longer be chased out of restaurants, minutes after enjoying our dessert. "No thanks, no check yet. We're after-dining."

Back to niksen. It could have been *nietsen*. Get a move on, stop nietsen! But it sounds too much like "Nietzsche" and would only cause confusion. Niksen sounds robust, like an activity. It has class, swagger. It sounds presidential—and I'm not talking about the soft, stinky cheese. I'm busy niksen! It sounds important, and so it is.

Lummelen and *lanterfanten* are other options, but are they any less negative? A *lummel* is a loser, a ne'er-do-well, a spineless bum, a wimp who's a waste of space. And *lummelen* is the verb based on it, so draw your own conclusions. How about the fun-sounding *lanterfanten*? The French *faire lanterner quelqu'un* means "to make somebody wait." Not exactly positive either. All right, let's look at the word's origins. With trepidation, we open our etymological dictionary again, hoping not to find something that dismisses niksen as chewing gum on the soles of society's shoes. We read that a *lanterfant* is somebody who "fritters away" his time, which is to say, wastes it on frivolities. The origins of the noun are "uncertain," but most likely we're dealing with a corruption of the word *land-trouwandt*, a hybrid of *land* and *trouwant*, meaning "beggar" or "vagabond." *Fant* could also derive from "infant." Again, it's not giving us warm fuzzy feelings.

How about the fun-sounding lanterfanten? The French faire lanterner quelqu'un means to make somebody wait. Not exactly positive either.

KLAPLOPERS

In the word *niksen* Dutch has a super-simple way to say doing nothing. But it also has a whole raft of nicknames for the people who do the idling. A *klaploper*, or "freeloader," is a good example. As with so many Dutch terms of abuse, it stems from a disease. If you suffered from a nasty infectious disease in the Middle Ages, nobody would hire you and you were forced to go out begging. People appreciated it if you heralded your arrival with a clapper, known as a *klap*, hence *klaploper*. It was a pretty antisocial solution to the problem: Give poor, sick people a clapper so you can hear them approach and hightail it if you didn't want to have anything to do with them. If only that annoying colleague from HR used one, then you could get away before she starts telling you all about her kids again. You wonder why the thing ever fell into disuse. Probably because we could never agree on who should carry a clapper, and eventually we'd all be tied to one and the streets would be filled with a deafening noise.

The first thing we thought of when *niksen* appeared on the global stage was a Dutch comedy show from the 1990s. To the best of our knowledge it was the first and last time the concept was discussed on national television—and it wasn't presented in a particularly positive light. In one episode, when forced to do nothing after a friend cancels a fun outing, one of the show's hosts confesses to falling into a black hole. Presumably the same black hole Blaise Pascal talked about: So much leisure time, but what to do with it? Don't spend it staring into space—that's when uncomfortable thoughts surface and the void beckons.

What the Dutch soccer player Johan Cruyff said about his sport can be said about niksen: Niksen is simple.

You can say what you like about the Dutch: They're direct, prone to complain, not averse to an argument, and their history is jam-packed with merchants, which is why they're supposedly tolerant (doesn't matter who you sell your products to, as long as you sell them) and good negotiators. They're the brains behind the renowned "polder model": negotiating until you drop or finally reach consensus (and you can start selling your goods again). But we wouldn't say niksen is prized. Sure, maybe after hours spent toiling in the garden, or after you've organized a local fundraiser, been to the gym, and also emptied the dishwasher—after all that, maybe you deserve a few minutes on the couch.

The nice thing about niksen is that it has no goal whatsoever. And yet we wrote this book to show you why niksen is good for you: It makes you calmer, because you allow your thoughts to just swirl around and give your crowded head a rest. It's good for your body, because it introduces a pause in what is probably a very hectic day. It increases your creativity, because it's when you're doing nothing that brilliant ideas pop into your head. And, finally, it's good for your wallet, because it's free. And so, we, too, were trapped in the tyranny of utility. While researching this subject it became clear that the best thing about niksen is the absence of a goal. It doesn't serve a purpose, but it's wonderful.

What the Dutch soccer player Johan Cruyff said about his sport can be said about niksen: Niksen is simple. The hardest thing is to simply do nothing. Not only does it have plenty of detractors, but it's also hard to pin down. For one, you can't plan it, because the whole point is to lose track of time. You have to remove something from your schedule and not add in something else. An evening spent binge-watching TV isn't niksen either. You may be chilling and not caught up in your own troubles for once, but you're gripped by those of others. It's a distraction, escapism. Spending a carefully timed half hour after dinner staring into space before you go about your plans for the evening—that's not niksen, either. Sitting on the couch, scrolling through social media and looking at photos, going into the kitchen to sneak a taste of whatever's cooking, leafing through a book, or messaging a friend is just more "whiling away the time": activities that are cognitively undemanding and don't have a deadline. Niksen is none of those things!

THE DEFINITION

Here's what it is: Niksen is suddenly, in an unguarded moment, having nothing to do and not finding something new to do. Or instead of doing an activity, niksen is canceling it and replacing it with absolutely nothing at all.

Niksen takes a bit of practice. Sometimes you almost slip into it, as if by accident, but then "gather" yourself again, either because you're bored or because you feel you ought to do something useful. The art of doing nothing lies in not letting yourself be governed by this learned behavior, but to continue to do nothing. You get there when you're staring apathetically at your computer and think there aren't enough hours in the day. When you've momentarily lost the plot and you suddenly find yourself staring out the window. You can't remember how you got there. Try to hold on to that sensation! If only for an instant. It's these moments—which cats probably enjoy all day long—that are so wonderful. The power of niksen is that there's nothing to it; it's a breeze.

The clock keeps ticking, but you don't have to watch it. Forget about it for a change.

This book is a hopeful attempt to turn niksen into an actual lifestyle. At a time when we're bombarded with obligations and expectations, and burnout, bore-out, and depression are on the rise, we think it's a good idea to bring in niksen as a momentary absence of time. The clock keeps ticking, but you don't have to watch it. Forget about it for a change. As the Zen saying goes, "You should sit in meditation for twenty minutes a day, unless you're too busy. Then you should sit for an hour."

We hope this has gotten you fired up about doing absolutely nada, and you're thinking to yourself, *Yes, please, give me that superpower to switch off*. There are three preconditions for doing nothing while feeling free from time: the aforementioned "having" of time, inner calm, and solitude.

BASIC INGREDIENTS

The three essential elements of niksen are: time, a calm mind, and a place where you won't be hassled.

It's an easy checklist. When you identify a moment for niksen—either because you've finished your work ahead of schedule or an appointment is unexpectedly canceled—run through this list:

- Can I stop checking my watch?
- Is my head relatively clear?
- Am I somewhere I can do nothing with reckless abandon?

Let's take a closer look at these three basic conditions.

1. Time

Rule number one: Stop watching the clock. In other words: There's no time limit. Like sex, you can't plan niksen. Of course, you technically could, but then it loses its spontaneity and becomes mechanical. You sacrifice its essence. Philosophical questions about time tend to remain unanswered. For instance, what exactly is time? Why do we talk about "wasting" or "stretching" time, when in actual fact time keeps going forward, consistently, as straight as it gets? How does time shape the way we live? Why is it that time seems to speed up every now and then? When it comes to niksen you have to ask yourself: Do you have the mental space to take everything you know about time and send it packing? To "lose" time, or at least to stop watching it? If your answer is yes, then you've cleared the first hurdle.

2. A calm mind

Ideally, you don't realize you're busy with niksen, so that, before you know it, minutes—even hours—have passed in which you were completely gone. It takes practice for you to fully accept that doing nothing has a place in this life. As a novice, you have to first check whether you have the inner calm and won't be distracted by all kinds of ruminations and other stimuli. When you've just downed your sixth cup of coffee, there's not much point in trying. It will be too much of an effort and you'll feel bad about yourself—and indirectly also about niksen—and throw in the towel, as you would with a diet that is so complex it requires you to consult a hefty book or complicated diagrams to see whether a food is permitted or not and you suddenly discover that you've accidentally eaten something forbidden.

Moments for niksen present themselves often enough, but you have to learn to recognize them. Lots of tasks on to-do lists can be deferred. It's great to cross things off so you end up with a blank slate, but postponing them isn't always wrong. Sometimes there's simply too much on your list. Emptying the dishwasher is a noble task, but you *could* just take the clean plates out as and when you need them. In some cases the kitchen cabinet can be skipped all together. And please don't work with reward systems, the kind where you ask yourself: Did I work hard enough today to let myself do nothing? The answer to that question is yes.

All right: Is your head clear? Yes? Great! Let's move on.

3. A good place

You're almost ready to surrender to the gods, to unbutton your pants and take a brief dip in infinite nothingness. The final hurdle is your environment. You can have people around, sure, but they should be totally on board with your just sitting in a corner. You can shift something like a chair here and there, but that's as far as it goes. It's okay if there's a colleague or a child nearby asking questions, but they mustn't judge you or make you feel like you are "wasting" your time. If that doesn't bother you, then great, but people giving you the side-eye can make niksen a lot harder. It's a bit like adolescents not wanting a parent on their case about homework and tests 24-7. We should all be on the same page. When someone close to you doesn't get it, show them this book.

As soon as these three conditions are met, you can embark on the big adventure that is niksen. We will show you what to do when you're struggling to get one or even all three to fall into place.

Welcome to the wondrous world of niksen.

1

Niksen and time

TOPICS

- The nature of time
- Why we are prisoners of time
- The exquisite lightness of doing nothing
- Niksen in company

Ask people about their memories of doing nothing and they often cite examples from childhood. How they woke up before their alarm, threw on some clothes, had a bite to eat, and then thought: What should I do today? Finish that drawing or convince my parents to get a dog? Children don't yet have a fully developed sense of time—instead adults keep track of it for them so they can forget about the concept altogether. But let's face it, as an adult you're always aware of the clock. You may experience moments outside time while on vacation, but how can you incorporate these into your daily life? How do you "lose" time so that you can briefly escape its grasp?

It's not easy to drop all your worries and responsibilities and to concentrate on nothing for half an hour or so. In fact, the whole point of niksen is that it doesn't become another agenda item. It's not supposed to be something to check off a list, just because a bunch of self-appointed lifestyle gurus say it's a trend and will make your heart ten years younger. Only once it's valued collectively can we all indulge in some undisturbed loafing without overthinking things.

The good news is that you're only one step away from niksen. All you need to do now is put down this book and try not to start a new activity. To help you on your way, the next two pages feature a really relaxing illustration.

THE QUESTION OF TIME

The Dutch philosopher Joke Hermsen is an advocate for a quieter life. Back in 2009, in the middle of the global financial crisis, she suggested that instead of working harder we should start doing less. For years now, she's been arguing in favor of a twenty-five-hour workweek. "It would instantly lower unemployment rates, rid us of a lot of stress and burn-out, and allow us to take better care of ourselves and the world. Why don't the experts come up with these kinds of visionary proposals instead of just 'more, more, more'?" she said in an interview in *Filosofie* magazine.

She would like to see people not cram their schedules with back-to-back appointments, and instead relax more often, aimlessly, without it necessarily leading somewhere—indulging in leisurely lounging that helps bring you clarity, or at least see things differently and change your mind. She has written several books about modern humans' relationship with time, about the way the clock rules our lives. Think of our set working hours. When we were children, at least we could decide for ourselves how long we spent on our homework, but at work every employee has to clock in and be present for a specific period of time, despite the fact that we don't all complete tasks at the same pace. It's weird to think that we're all expected to keep going for eight, nine, or more hours, when we can be mentally absent for long stretches at a time. And yet the time when we're spaced out isn't monitored.

A SENSE OF MORTALITY

Human beings know that their time here on Earth is limited, that one day it will all end. This is both a blessing and a curse. We learn to intensely savor the happy moments, but we fear life ebbing away. We ask ourselves what will happen when we die, but those are uncomfortable thoughts, and so off we go, seeking distraction again. As a result, "wasting" time is looked down upon. We think: *Life is short, you never know when it's going to end, so make the most of it! Live your best life!* Knowing that this life is finite is a gift; that's why we know we have to enjoy it until we're running on empty. It's a paradox: Life is beautiful, dying less so, yet it's death that makes life more beautiful, or at least special. Squandering that life by doing nothing except hanging around is not an option.

Meditation existed thousands of years ago.
Since then we may have made good progress in countless
areas, but we're still no good at niksen.

In 2018 the physicist Alan Lightman published *In Praise of Wasting Time*, in which he extolls the virtues of not doing anything useful with your time, of having what he describes as "unstructured time with no goal." Lunch with a friend can therefore be seen as a waste of time—unless you're meeting because you want to ask your friend for a loan or advice or something. Lightman stresses that people have been trying to find peace and quiet, chill out, and reduce all this crazy stress for centuries. Meditation existed thousands of years ago. Since then we may

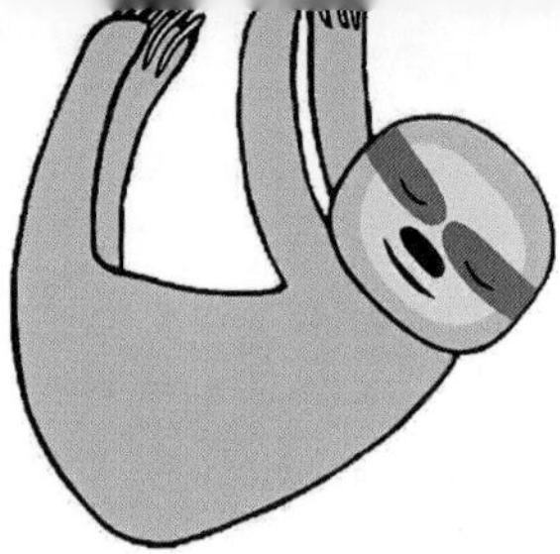

have made good progress in countless areas, but we're still no good at niksen.

Lightman cites some interesting studies in his book, including one jointly carried out by the University of Virginia and Harvard, in which students were told to sit alone in a room for twelve minutes, without external stimuli. The room was empty except for a button that, if pressed, would administer an electric shock. After testing it once, the subjects all commented that it was unpleasant, something they would avoid at all costs. There were two rules: They weren't allowed to fall asleep or to get out of their chair. In the end, 67 percent of the men and 25 percent of the women chose to shock themselves. Is doing nothing simply not in our nature? The French philosopher Blaise Pascal claimed that "all of humanity's problems stem from man's inability to sit quietly in a room alone."

The French philosopher Blaise Pascal claimed that "all of humanity's problems stem from man's inability to sit quietly in a room alone."

Lightman concludes:

> Since the digital screen has replaced reality and has become the architect of our intimacies, we will always fear aloneness. We will find it next to impossible to sit in a quiet room by ourselves and figure out who we are. The biggest thing we're missing out on is, in fact, ourselves.

You need time for niksen, for thinking about things and feeling almost bored—for learning who you are.

HANGIN' IN THE ANIMAL KINGDOM

In the animal kingdom, doing nothing is held in high regard. It looks perfect: lots of sleep, the occasional hunt for your dinner, and then straight back to your nest.

We humans are the only species to have turned time into a measurable concept. Animals have relaxation down to a T, but the drawback is that they haven't managed to defeat their natural enemies as effectively—and they're not big on self-development or dealing with trauma. As an animal, growing up is a matter of survival rather than living your best life. We often envy our pets for the way they while away the time. How on Earth do they do that? No self-awareness, that helps. Free food and accommodation, that's useful, too. But is there anything we can learn from our furry friends?

Let's start by looking at the sloth. This clingy creature sleeps ten hours a day. Not all that much! Because it's so slow, the sloth consumes hardly any energy. That brings us to the first disadvantage: A sloth can eat only very little, otherwise it would grow too fat and fall out of its tree. Another downside is that every now and then they have to leave the branch they're hanging from to defecate. For this they go to a place where all sloths go to poop. And here's the biggest drawback of all: That spot is also where couples meet. Their cruising ground, you could say. They do this about once a week. Not ideal, but perhaps there's something to be said for seeing your prospective partner at their worst. So if you're someone with even a scrap of ambition, you wouldn't want to adopt any of the sloth's attributes. Not eating is antisocial, and meeting your partner on your own dung heap isn't going to be the next Tinder either. The same holds true for koalas: They sleep the best part of the day and only nibble on eucalyptus. Eating is incredibly important to people. It's a great source of happiness and vitality, and it's a fun, social activity. For us, these things are absolutely nonnegotiable.

FEELING BORED

Niksen has many foes—boredom or the fear of boredom among them. We can't spend the whole day just hanging or lying around. That's what cats, sloths, and other creatures do.

There's a (perhaps fine) line between niksen and feeling bored. When you do nothing for too long, you might get bored. Is that really such a bad thing, though? It's almost impossible for people in this day and age to be bored, because we have so much entertainment to digest. When was the last time you were on a train or in a waiting room without six different types of media clamoring for your attention with their beautiful and "urgent" content? While a toddler is running around screaming because he has a pea stuck up his nose, his parent is totally engrossed in the life of drug lords in an underground system of tunnels in Mexico. The only challenge you face is staring down the disapproving looks of the folks who complain that "people have no time for each other anymore." To the British psychologist Sandi Mann, who wrote the book *The Science of Boredom*, it's "the curse of the twenty-first century; it seems that the more we have to stimulate us, the more stimulation we crave. . . . We are losing the ability to tolerate the routine and repetition of everyday life." It means that if we want silence, we must actively seek it out, for instance by taking vacations without cell phones or booking silent retreats.

To Mann, boredom doesn't stem from being unable to come up with an activity that has some minimal function, but from the inability to think of something you enjoy doing. Not doing anything at all is only possible if you're in solitary confinement and have already pleasured yourself three times and muscle ache is preventing you from a fourth attempt. Even getting off loses its appeal after a while. Boredom is frustrating because of dissatisfaction with your circumstances. According to Mann, we can't allow this boredom to continue, so we try to alleviate it with "empty" activities like online shopping or silly games. Funnily enough, men are bored with online shopping after only twenty-six minutes, whereas for women it takes two hours before the tedium kicks in. What?!

Mann gives talks based on her book and describes how, as a rule, 99 percent of her audience admits to feeling bored from time to time. "But there is always one person who raises their hand and asserts proudly that they are NEVER bored," she writes. "Whether this is true or not (I suspect that they simply have excellent coping mechanisms for boredom rather than never experiencing it), the implication for everyone else is clear: only the inactive, lazy and feeble-minded get bored."

Funnily enough, men are bored with online shopping after only twenty-six minutes, whereas for women it takes two hours before the tedium kicks in. What?!

Peter Toohey, a professor of Greek and Roman studies, concluded his research into boredom by saying that some people are more easily bored than others due to the levels of dopamine produced by the brain. He also argues that boredom can be healthy, as it can act as an early warning sign that certain situations may be harmful. And while you're feeling bored—when you're in a lecture hall, for instance, listening to a dull speaker—you could begin to daydream, which in turn could spark creativity. Those who call themselves "intellectual" refer to boredom as "ennui" and then it's an existential thing. According to Nietzsche, creatives require a lot of boredom to achieve their best work. He described boredom as "the unpleasant calm of the soul" that precedes the "dancing breezes" of creativity. It causes some discomfort, but eventually you reap the benefits. Nietzsche loathed people who trundled off to work every day simply because they had to. It was imposed on them from an impressionable age, and that's why they now deserve three or four weeks of vacation every year. Ridiculous, he thought. In *The Dawn of Day* he wrote that these "beasts of burden" would rise up if deprived of their "'holidays,' . . . this ideal of leisure in an overworked century . . . in which they may for once be idle, idiotic, and childish to their heart's content."

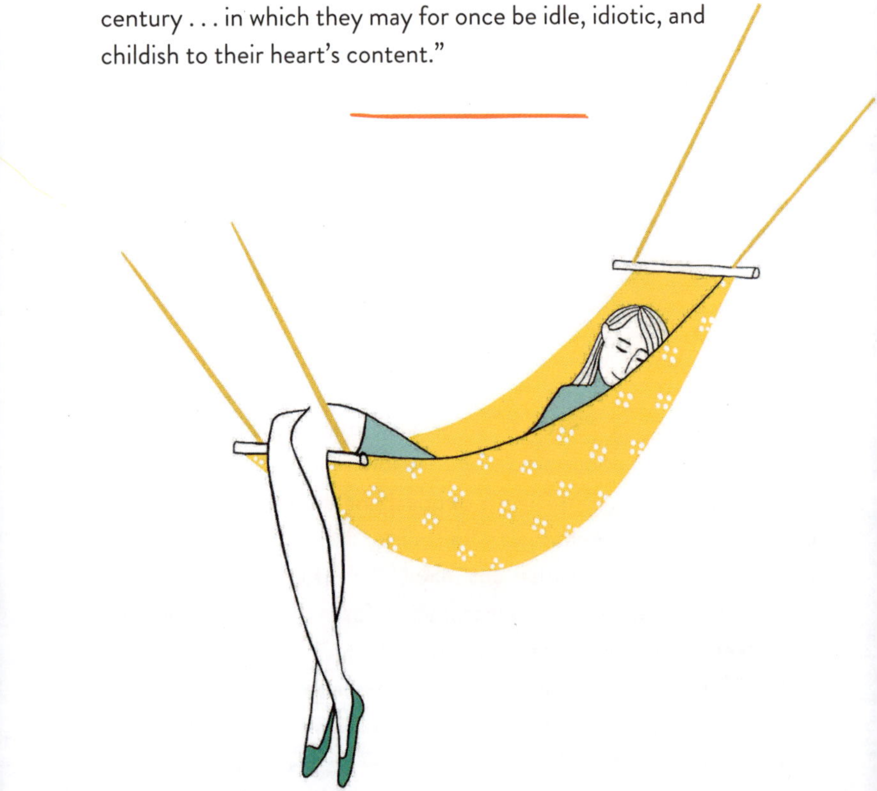

NIKSEN LIKE A BUTTERFLY

The Dutch philosopher Awee Prins has been researching boredom since his doctoral studies. In his writings on the subject he cites the poem *Het uur u* (H hour) by the Dutch poet Martinus Nijhoff:

> a calm, not just in form
> a calm before the storm,
> but a calm of the sort
> in which things are received
> that were never perceived before.

Awee believes we would be able to see and hear this different, calm world if only we weren't so busy drowning out silence and fighting boredom. In a wide-ranging conversation we had with Awee, he suggested that boredom is a sign of dissatisfaction; most people try to avoid it. "But niksen is the sunny side of boredom," he said. For those who are consistently hard workers, like the Dutch, it's hard to relax—and especially difficult to do nothing. "We're fascinated by anyone who manages to escape the rat race and do nothing. Odes to idleness and other such controversial fare are what you'd expect to find in France." After all, Awee said, it was a Frenchman, Paul Lafargue—Karl Marx's son-in-law—who wrote *The Right to Be Lazy*, in which he challenges his father-in-law by arguing for a shorter working day. You would never have heard this argument from someone Dutch.

The question remains: Are human beings capable of doing nothing? Interestingly, Awee pointed out, "Our word *school* derives from the Ancient Greek *scholè*, which literally means 'leisure'—time when you don't have to do anything." Our curiosity thrives in leisure. "The Greeks began to feed their curiosity, explore this wondrous world, and examine themselves. Think of Socrates, arguing that 'the unexamined life is not worth living.' As a result, the Greeks were bad at taking time off. We have the Sabbath, or Sunday, a day set aside for rest, which is sweet after labor. Leisure time and doing nothing are always something you have to earn, a gift to be grateful for. It's something we see in Christianity: Niksen is idleness, and idle hands are the devil's workshop. The Dutch are particularly afflicted by this. When you do nothing, you're not productive, but lazy and wicked. We can't shake off twenty-five centuries of not knowing what to do with time off." If only it were that easy!

It's something we see in Christianity: Niksen is idleness, and idle hands are the devil's workshop.

Maybe that's why we're so desperate to tackle malingering at work and phenomena like stress and burnout. We want to cure them right away, as we would want to smooth over a pothole in the road and make use of an empty building, even if only temporarily, through a pop-up shop. In his research Awee suggests that many recent movements and lifestyle trends that promote slow living have developed in response to our broader social climate—for instance, hippies who lived by "'turn on, tune in, drop out," or the global Slow Movement described by Carl Honoré, who promotes slow food, slow sex, slow cities. These trends urge us to resist acceleration, to shift down a gear. But slowing down isn't entirely new, Awee says. Every ten or twenty years there's a new buzzword to help us put up with stress, and those ideas quickly become overdone. Trends react to social movement and keep us engaged in our lives—just keep calm and carry on. "What's great about the word *niksen* is that it's so brazen," said Awee, "representing a way of moving like a butterfly in that strange space between being and not being, and perhaps even between life and death, and that makes it truly fascinating." It's vital that we don't also turn niksen into something with purpose. Niksen starts and ends with nothing. There's nothing to it and we should keep it that way.

As you might expect, niksen has many foes. There's boredom, but also the danger that others find it morally reprehensible or think you're lazy. "Like any adventure, as soon as it turns dangerous it stops being fun," says Awee. But we know better. "You have to get into the spirit of niksen itself, and the beauty of it is that, unlike a vacation or an excursion, it's not finite." Obviously, as soon as you feel hungry your niksen will come to a natural conclusion. "But niksen has this intrinsic ability to confront us with nothingness in a very lighthearted, free, and easy way. While fear also confronts us with nothingness, it takes a superdramatic, unpleasant approach. We panic, realize we're mortal, and then want to get even more out of life." A bit of naysaying never hurt a good philosophy—and might even strengthen it. We've come to expect the opposition.

As our conversation wrapped up, Awee suggested, "The beauty of niksen is that it's casual and a lot more ephemeral, yet in a strange way still connects us with pure being. Not being in the sense of doing, or developing, or reaching, but pure being. Niksen is aimed at nothing in particular and that's why it's perceived as an insignificant and inconsequential phenomenon. But perhaps that's what makes it so amazingly beautiful and interesting: It may seem unremarkable, yet strangely enough niksen truly connects you with everything. With everything and nothing. But then we must not elevate niksen to a pause from which we emerge stronger and more creative. The goal is not to optimize our experience, like previous trends. Instead, we must learn to remain close to niksen itself."

BUT WHAT ABOUT MY SCHEDULE?

Schedules are a necessary evil. You can't be expected to memorize every single one of your appointments. But the good news is that you're the one responsible for planning your calendar. Angela Maas, a cardiologist, says we must learn to "park" our commitments so our heart doesn't give out. One of her tips is to write down all of your tasks so you're not constantly running through them in your head. Checking tasks off your to-do list is a great feeling—it's even rewarding to list a few you've already completed, so you can cross them out right away. Green checks for the win!

Georgia Holt, the mother of singer, Oscar-winning actress, and overall icon Cher, gave her daughter this useful tip: "If it doesn't matter in five years, it doesn't matter." Many of your problems are temporary and virtually forgotten tomorrow or next week. You may wonder whether a colleague at work hates you. It may even give you sleepless nights. But once you know that she's short-tempered with everyone, you stop thinking about it. Many worries disappear naturally, and you find that all the energy you put in is wasted.

Man often suffers most
from the adversity he fears
but never actually appears.
Thus has he more to bear
than God in His wisdom thinks fair.
—Nicolaas Beets, nineteenth-century
Dutch theologian

STOP the GLORIFICATION of your SCHEDULE

BUSY BUSY
BUSY BUSY
BUSY BUSY

FALLING VICTIM TO PERFECTIONISM

Perfectionism is time-consuming. If you're aiming for perfection, a job is never done because nothing can ever be flawless. That's why perfectionism is an enemy of niksen. The bestselling author Brené Brown has written extensively about accepting your own imperfections. In *Daring Greatly* she identifies the common fear that you're not good enough and should be called out for not doing all you could for your job or relationship, and impostor syndrome, which makes you feel you don't deserve your success and are only a hair's breadth away from being found out. In response, Brown urges people to "own their story" and not be ashamed of who they are. That includes not trying to do everything at once. As Brown puts it, practice self-compassion. Perfectionism is other-focused (how will I be judged?), but healthy striving is self-focused.

TIP

You often know well in advance that your calendar is too full. Don't wait to cancel appointments: Give plenty of notice, so the other person has enough time to plan something new and so that you don't feel bad about it.

SLEEP DEPRIVATION

Some people swear by eight hours or more; others claim they can get by on just a few hours a night. For years, it's been a worrying trend: Politicians and businesspeople boasting of sleeping only four hours before getting up again to save the world. It creates this false idea that sleep is for losers and that it gets in the way of success. "I'll sleep when I'm dead"—that kind of thing. Ironically, you're more likely to die when you suffer from chronic sleep deprivation. Some people get up at 4:00 AM and run for an hour because it reduces their stress. That's great, but hopefully they take a few naps during the day. Then there are the early birds. Dolly Parton doesn't get much shut-eye because, as she says, her "metabolism just doesn't require a lot of sleep." She says five hours of sleep is a lot for her; she goes to bed early, rising again three hours after midnight. She also takes a nap after lunch but loves the peace and quiet in the morning and gets all her work done during the "wee hours."

Dolly Parton doesn't get much shut-eye because, as she says, her "metabolism just doesn't require a lot of sleep." She says five hours of sleep is a lot for her; she goes to bed early, rising again three hours after midnight.

Sleep is important. In his book *Why We Sleep*, Matthew Walker, a neuroscientist, criticizes the popularity of skipping on sleep. Walker writes, "Sleep *before* learning refreshes our ability to initially make new memories. It does so each and every night. While we are awake, the brain is constantly acquiring and absorbing novel information." Centuries ago, people would sleep for four hours at night, get up to do some work, and go back to bed for another four hours. Walker also indicates that sleep deprivation contributes to poor workplace performance and irritable bosses. To prove just how damaging it is, he cites the example of sleep deprivation as a torture method. After being kept awake for days on end, people confess to the most horrible crimes when promised uninterrupted sleep. Walker describes a lack of sleep as "a slow form of self-euthanasia . . . one of the greatest public health challenges we face in the twenty-first century in developed nations," and calls for radical changes in society. We must make sleep cool again, strip it of "embarrassment or the damaging stigma of laziness. In doing so, we can be reunited with that most powerful elixir of wellness and vitality."

NAPS

What about naps of fifteen minutes or less? We're all familiar with that nodding-off feeling in the afternoon. That moment during a meeting when everybody suddenly agrees—"Yes, that's it, that's the way forward!"—and you have no idea what they're talking about, because you were dreaming of sun, sea, and sand. You nod and hope someone sends around detailed minutes. The biological urge to nap in the afternoon, a form of postprandial hypotension (aka food coma), is no longer indulged in our daily routine. But when drowsiness strikes, people are less alert. Should you ever want to force a brilliant idea down the throats of reluctant colleagues, the afternoon is the ideal time to do so—success not always guaranteed.

TIPS FOR A GOOD NIGHT'S SLEEP

Luckily, a growing number of people are now calling for more sleep. Arianna Huffington, CEO of *HuffPost*, is on board. Her chronic sleep deprivation was so bad she once fainted from exhaustion, prompting a major rethink. Now, with her book *The Sleep Revolution*, she's trying to convince people to sleep for the recommended eight hours a night, with six simple tips:

1. Switch off your devices thirty minutes before you go to bed.
2. Take a bath before you go to bed.
3. Put on your PJs.
4. Keep your bedroom cool, dark, and quiet.
5. Don't drink caffeine after 2:00 PM.
6. Only use your bed for sleep and sex.

TAKING NAPS sounds so CHILDISH

I PREFER to call them

HORIZONTAL LIFE PAUSES

In an ideal world, your employer would encourage you to nap in a bed or on a comfy couch or beanbag chair. "Power naps" are now all the rage. The effects of a fifteen-minute nap last up to three hours. Thomas Edison, a man who had a million ideas a minute and who barely slept, enjoyed naps, too. In fact, he attributed his genius to them. Whenever he was stuck, he took a trip to dreamland for a creative boost. Salvador Dalí also swore by a snooze. These are useful names to drop when you'd like to doze off at work.

Naps are all about the sleep cycle. It's imperative that you not wake up when you're in your deepest REM sleep. That would be counter-productive. Companies like Google and Nike have already introduced some more flexibility into their workweeks to accommodate both night owls and early birds. Whether or not their employees make use of this flexibility isn't known. Perhaps we need a culture shift first. At NASA, however, naps are perfectly normal. Following extensive research they discovered that the best nap length is twenty-six minutes.

When drowsiness strikes, people are less alert. Should you ever want to force a brilliant idea down the throats of reluctant colleagues, the afternoon is the ideal time to do so—success not always guaranteed.

NIKSEN AND FAMILY

It can be wonderful to move at someone else's pace for a while, precisely because it leaves you free to forget the time. To kids, the summer vacation sometimes feels too long(!?). They miss their usual routine. That's unimaginable to most grownups, who, even when on vacation, have lost the ability to relax to the point of boredom. What once felt terrible is now something we look back on with nostalgia.

As a child, you live your parents' life to some extent. They even take you along to the birthday parties of their friends—people you don't always care about or in some cases even dislike. Remember all those times when you were left to play with a bunch of strange children? You weren't happy about it at all, but by the time your parents were ready to go home you were actually having a fun afternoon. You were completely absorbed in your game and didn't want to be wrenched away. Much snickering from your parents ensued: "What do you mean you don't want to go? You didn't even want to come along!" Once again, you had no choice but to get back in the car, because their lives determined yours. As an adult, you sometimes don't like your own plans, but when you're a child, it's part of life and you just have to accept it. You may put up a fight from time to time, but you grow up and eventually gain your independence. When you develop into a well-adjusted adult, you learn to express the frustrations of your inner child in a healthy way. Imagine that your partner has to attend a Christmas party dressed as a reindeer and expects you to accompany them as an elf. You will resist with every fiber of your being. But you love your partner and so you put on those pointy shoes and make the best of a bad situation.

It can be wonderful to move at someone else's pace for a while, precisely because it leaves you free to forget the time.

By voluntarily immersing yourself in another person's busy life for a day you can take your mind off your own concerns. You go to the hardware store with your partner, pick up a birthday cake, buy a new lampshade for Grandma, and help to redecorate her living room. You're not doing nothing, but you have opened the door to not doing anything that's directly useful to yourself. After dragging Grandma's heavy bookcase across the room, you may suddenly find yourself standing with a cup of tea in your hand, gazing at two butterflies flitting around. Perhaps you even experience one of those wonderful middle-distance stares you can lose yourself in.

Another form of niksen with family involves withdrawing from them. Remember those times when you managed to escape your parents' watchful eye as a child—or thought you did—and you had that feeling of momentarily not existing, because you didn't have to be anyone or go anywhere?

You're not doing nothing, but you have opened the door to not doing anything that's directly useful to yourself.

NIKSEN AND FRIENDS

It's not just a busy work schedule that fills up before you realize it; your social life can also become too much. So the question is: Is it possible to niksen with friends?

Who better than friends?! If you're close to a friend, you know you can take a three-hour nap on their couch without inviting ridicule. You don't care what they think of it and you know they'll tell you if they want the couch for themselves. You probably take the best naps on your best friend's couch. However, you usually plan to meet your friends so that you can catch up, and not just watch them doze off, or fall asleep yourself. Yes, struggling to stay awake when you're tired is hard work, and we know that sleep deprivation can cause terrible problems, but if napping is all that's going down, you might as well have stayed at home. Of course, you don't *have* to take a nap, but it's nice to know that your friendship has the necessary room for it if you *were* to fall asleep. And that space is what niksen with friends is all about: being silent together and letting your mind wander. You can only really do absolutely nothing *with* somebody when you have both fully embraced the concept of niksen. That said, it's great to be aimless with friends: shooting the breeze, eating, lying on the couch, and doing precious little.

In popular culture, friends are often depicted as people you can call day or night to talk about all of your problems, however big or small. For proper niksen with friends it's vital that you know them really well, that they're more than just casual friends. The British psychologist Sue Johnson, who's known for her book *Hold Me Tight* and who developed emotionally focused therapy (EFT), writes that people seldom add making new friends or establishing closer friendships to their list of New

Year's resolutions. We care more about the number of people attending our birthday party than the closeness of those people. How ridiculous! It's better to deepen existing friendships, and according to Johnson doing so must be a conscious choice. Dr. Amir Levine, a neuroscientist who teaches at Columbia University, has formulated five foundational elements of secure relationships: consistency, availability, reliability, responsiveness, and predictability. With these five components in place, you can deepen a relationship with someone and be able to do nothing together. For example, with reliability you don't have to worry that your friend will be bored by your company. And with responsiveness, you'll be so attuned to each other that you'll know when something goes too far.

QUIET PARTY
Two o'clock. My place. Casual dress code, because we'll do nothing. Except maybe have something to eat. Love to see you.
invitation

#JOMO

Friendships are important, but it's possible to have too many. According to Robin Dunbar, an anthropologist, you only need five close ones. With too many friends, you have too many group chats, too many drinks scheduled after work, too many parties at the weekend, and potential vacation plans. When popularity becomes exhausting, it's nice to embrace the joy of missing out (aka JOMO).

You don't often hear people say, I've got tickets for a sold-out festival this weekend, but I'm not going. Bliss! And yet canceling plans can feel liberating.

There are a thousand and one things you can do in your leisure time, but is too much choice stressing you out and giving you FOMO (fear of missing out)? Then why not swap FOMO for JOMO? You don't often hear people say, I've got tickets for a sold-out festival this weekend, but I'm not going. Bliss! And yet canceling plans can feel liberating. As with niksen, you remove something from your to-do list. Picture it as a heavy backpack: After a long journey with lots of nearly missed connections and bad weather you can finally let it slip off your shoulders. However fun your plans may be, sometimes it's even better to put on your PJs and do as you goddamn please. Social media isn't exactly flooded with photos of people lying on the couch in a snug onesie. Never mind perfect images in your feed and be as lazy as possible for a change.

NIKSEN ON VACATION

Vacations and niksen are a match made in heaven. Some people set their alarm clocks while on vacation, though in principle it's the perfect time to do nothing. Beware of the potential pitfalls: You may feel you *have to* relax. Since it's the only time of the year when you're allowed to loaf around, that could open the door to stress and obligations. After all, vacation is your time to recharge and enjoy ultimate relaxation. If you're lucky and have managed to secure three consecutive weeks off, you may feel pressure to find the Great Relaxation. Another hazard comes when vacationing with friends, or meeting others while away—as we've learned from Jean-Paul Sartre, hell is other people. Like you, those other people only have a few weeks for a complete reset. Add to this that it's the one time when we can finally visit all those countries on our bucket list, and we can wave goodbye to relaxation. Let's see the world! It's supposed to be fun and carefree, but traveling almost never is.

If you're lucky and have managed to secure three consecutive weeks off, you may feel pressure to find the Great Relaxation.

We all have different ideas about the perfect vacation. Some like to crisscross entire continents with only a backpack; others pack three large suitcases and never leave their five-star luxury resort. Then there are those who enjoy a staycation and the occasional day trip. In any event you must not forget about niksen, especially when you're in another country with new cultures, food, and architecture, or home with stacks of books clamoring for your attention. When you're on vacation,

it's the ideal time to say, "And now it's time for absolutely nothing." So how do you go about it?

Great locations are a major pitfall when traveling: idyllic beaches, gorgeous panoramas, unique natural phenomena, the best and the most beautiful the world has to offer! The northern lights, a private villa on a pristine white beach, the salt flats of Bolivia, or the stunning landscape of Vietnam. Amazing destinations, each and every one of them, but the pressure to go and see all that beauty and to respond to it in an authentic way is immense. It's tempting to cram in as many activities as possible, because you don't want to miss out if this is your only visit to a particular country. If you're still hungover from a Thai Full Moon Party, you won't want to schlep through the surf to a nearby island when all you can think of is your hammock and that nagging headache. Bear this in mind when you plan your vacation, and take it easy. Do you really think it would be fun to visit all the highlights during a week in New York City?! You don't hear many people say: "I was in Paris, and OMG that Eiffel Tower is a-ma-zing." Or "How I loved Trafalgar Square." These are tourist traps that locals tend to shun. Meanwhile, you may go around the city with a guidebook in hand, checking off the supposed highlights.

We love this message from an interview with Godfried Bomans, a Dutch author, about a tourist visiting London Bridge: "Do you know who sees that bridge? The local Londoner who's going to buy sausages across the river, because they're cheaper over there. He crosses that bridge and he uses that bridge and he sees it in passing. Like a by-product. Like an extra. That's the real seeing." Meanwhile the visitor can't see the bridge with an open mind, because he's comparing it to the guidebook entry. Looking at it that way, you should take your hangover and walk away from that Thai island—you should be more concerned with getting rid of your headache than with the beauty of the island. If you walk away, then the island would be the by-product and you would have a functional relationship with it. You're not just there to drink in the experience.

If you see your destination as a new place to live your life and do whatever you feel like doing, then you're off to a good, relaxing start. The former queen of the Netherlands, Princess Beatrix, clearly has it all figured out. She goes skiing in Lech, Austria, every winter and spends her summers in a villa in Italy. The gossip magazines have been writing about it for years, and no doubt most of the stories aren't true, but we're left with an image of a princess making sculptures in the Tuscan sun, accompanied by her dogs. Because she's been going to the same place since the 1970s, she has no desire to visit picturesque churches and other local landmarks. Not everybody has the good fortune of being gifted a gorgeous house by a wealthy count, or the money to pay for one, but the concept is simple: Avoid stimuli or the pressure to go out and explore—or at least keep them to a minimum.

We all have different ideas about the perfect vacation. Some like to crisscross entire continents with only a backpack; others pack three large suitcases and never leave their five-star luxury resort.

PRACTICAL TIPS:

Where do you find the time?

Your child won't stop texting you, you're hurtling out of a work meeting and your head is spinning, and when you get home you have to produce yet another family dinner, take your pet hamster to therapy, and squeeze in a visit to the gym. Time is the biggest obstacle to niksen. More and more often the question "How are you doing?" is followed by "Are you busy?" Sometimes the latter replaces the former altogether. Everybody is busy, so you must be, too.

If you want time to do nothing, you have to set it aside in your head. You need to flip that switch: the famous off switch. Before you blow a fuse. The OFF switch! Because you can't always be ON. The off switch is the final stop before burnout. STOP, another word for: Watch out! Drop everything. Now.

Stop praising the virtues of a full schedule

Nobody used to ask adults, let alone children, whether they were busy. But these days it's not all that strange to ask a nine-year-old child whether they're managing to fit it all in. Emotional exhaustion is being diagnosed in ever-younger people. In 2019, the Netherlands Youth Institute estimated that 4 to 8 percent of children aged eight to twelve suffer from anxiety or mood disorders. We need to halt this train!

You can start by not overfilling your schedule and by creating a bit of space for niksen instead. When you make plans, ask yourself: Do I really need to do this? When the answer is no: Drop it. Don't meet up with people you don't like; don't systematically work overtime. We allow our schedules to dictate the way we live our lives. Some people even plan their hedonism. Working people go absolutely berserk on the weekends so they can be their usual well-behaved selves when they go back to the office on Monday morning.

TIP

Don't cram too much into your schedule. Try to clear your calendar for a day. And if a full day isn't realistic, try a half. Plan to do your grocery shopping and social stuff in the morning and plan nothing, sweet nothing, from 1:00 PM onward.

I hate housework.
You make the beds.
You do the dishes.
And six months later you
have to start all over again.
joan rivers

One step at a time

Human beings take their time to learn to walk, well over a year. Babies might be able to see everybody running around all day, but they're too busy with other developments. They need to accept the fact that they won't be carried around for the rest of their lives! Under huge social pressure, they take their first tentative steps. At first, a child waddles like a drunk sumo wrestler, and when they're fed up or tired they're carried again. It will likewise take some time, but we can turn doing nothing into a habit that's stored in our body and becomes a procedural memory, which—like walking—we never forget.

Don't expect immediate results. You won't just fall into blissful, stimulus-free Zen moments. It takes time to grow this skill. At first, try for a brief moment every day. Sit down and don't come up with a dozen new tasks to complete. Look around you. And if you don't manage to settle into doing nothing, don't sweat it. It's okay to fail and attempt it again tomorrow. If you do achieve a moment of niksen, try to make this moment last a little longer each time.

There's no need to immediately find a particular outlet for doing nothing. For some it takes the shape of doodling, for others it's staring out the window. If it's totally meaningless, it's niksen.

Feel your muscles

It helps to learn how to put the brakes on your runaway train of thought. Stopping it completely is hard, but at the very least you can slow it down. Anyone who's ever done yoga knows that the end relaxation often consists of appreciating the body you've just put through a workout. The instructor will encourage you to release the tension from your body by observing all of your muscles. You can visualize them as valves and open them to let out the tension like air from a balloon. If you're unable to switch off your thoughts, try to return to the here and now by flexing your muscles one by one and then relaxing them again.

Give your emotions a place

If you're not in touch with your body, you can check in with your emotions. What's that tight knot in your stomach? Is it anger? Or is it another emotion? What exactly does it feel like, where does it begin and where does it end? Don't try to put the feeling into words and don't try to find a cause. Concentrate long enough and it will take on another form. With a bit of luck that emotion will shrink and eventually disappear.

2

Niksen and your body

TOPICS

- **The pace of life could be making you sick**
- **The effect of stress on your heart**
- **How to escape the rat race**

In addition to a peaceful mind, niksen requires a body capable of doing absolutely nothing at all. But as Oscar Wilde said, "It is awfully hard work doing nothing." And why is it so hard? Because our head gets in the way. The greatest internal stumbling blocks are the ingrained ideas about how you should live your life and the many fears you have to conquer to go against those ideas. These thoughts lead to stress and even burnout. In this chapter we'll survey and account for important parts of the body.

STRESS

Let's start at the top, with the head. People often think that niksen is something they have to "earn," that staring contentedly into space can only follow from an honest day's work. Shuffling straight from the bed to the couch doesn't feel quite right. It must be *allowed*—and that's all in your mind. Nobody is keeping score, at least not down here on Earth. Throughout the ages, people have been asking themselves: Am I working too hard? Is it possible to have a good work–life balance? And why is there so much work to do outside of working hours and under terrible conditions? Why can't we just live in paradise somewhere, with treats and naps aplenty, instead of spending eight hours a day with colleagues who don't know how to work the printer? Humans are inventing better and faster devices, and yet our workload only seems to increase. You'd think that all these machines would allow us to take it easy, but instead we have growing mental health problems, and burnout is on the rise.

Is it possible to calm our brains by removing stimuli from our environment? In the 1920s, the German psychiatrist and neurologist Hans Berger, who invented the EEG (electroencephalogram, which shows brain waves on paper), discovered that the human brain is always active, even when asleep or doing nothing. At rest, our brains use only 5 percent less energy. Your brain is always on, which can be maddening.

Stress is a foe of niksen. Like depression, it's an umbrella concept, which needs unfolding: Stress doesn't necessarily spring from a lack of relaxation, nor is it always a bad thing. In fact, drinking endless cups of coffee may well have the same physical effect as the stress you experience at work. Also, some stress triggers are imaginary. You can drive yourself crazy imagining the many things that could go wrong during a presentation, and it can just as easily go off without a hitch. As the French philosopher Michel de Montaigne said, "He who fears he shall suffer, already suffers what he fears."

The psychiatrist Witte Hoogendijk and the journalist Wilma de Rek have charted the history of stress, and outline four types of stressors:

1. **Concrete and acute** (a lion about to tear you to shreds)
2. **Concrete and chronic** (the earth on the verge of overheating)
3. **Abstract and acute** (a nasty thought that suddenly pops into your head: Maybe your house is on fire because a paper napkin has fluttered onto a sandwich maker. Did you remember to switch it off? Do you have insurance?)
4. **Abstract and chronic** (the constant feeling that you're falling short in every way).

The fourth is the biggest culprit in causing stress, because it can drive people completely insane—and it's hard to switch it off. Hoogendijk and De Rek also suggest that the number of stressors in category 4 has risen exponentially in the past century. While humankind needed millions of years to develop into the *Homo sapiens* we are now, for much of that time we made no progress to speak of. But during the Industrial Revolution (circa 1760), life stressors increased exponentially. However, our body hasn't developed any new stress responses in the last five hundred million years—from a physiological perspective, we pretty much stopped evolving at that point. All we can do now is modify our behavior by harnessing the power of technology, listening to our body, and going into nature to recharge our battery. Think of it as the polder model in action (see page 13).

BURNOUT

Lots of stress can result in burnout symptoms or even total incapacity. The number of people suffering from burnout is skyrocketing; many people are overworked and exhausted or have had to take mental health leave from work before the age of thirty. A Dutch report on well-being in the workplace found that in the space of a decade the number of people experiencing symptoms of burnout rose from 11 to 16 percent. And the end is not yet in sight. To make matters worse, the average age of people suffering from burnout is going down. A study carried out by the Netherlands Youth Institute found that 4 to 8 percent of children under twelve suffer from anxiety and mood disorders. Among children aged thirteen and over, 10 percent were found to have an anxiety disorder. If we continue at this rate, we'll soon all be dead on our feet.

The term *burnout* was coined in 1974 by Herbert Freudenberger, a research psychologist. Having examined a group of volunteers at an addiction clinic, he concluded that they had developed symptoms of depression in response to feeling powerless. Initially, the phenomenon was mainly diagnosed in people working in the care and education sectors, but now it's everywhere. It has also been officially recognized by the World Health Organization (WHO) as a medical condition.

We are all different, living different lives, and having different responses to stressful problems. There is no ready-made solution.

It's telling that in today's world these reports elicit vastly different reactions, ranging from "It's really not that bad" to headlines like

BURNOUT EPIDEMIC COSTING ECONOMY BILLIONS. Whom should we believe? Those who say stress is ever-present, that this is nothing new? Or those who claim it's destroying us? As is so often the case, the truth is somewhere in the middle. Christiaan Vinkers, a psychiatrist who studies stress, offers a level-headed approach: Yes, many people struggle to find a satisfying work–life balance, and in many cases it leads people to be checked out. He also believes that more research into burnout is needed to get a better handle on the subject. According to Vinkers, it's unlikely that people are experiencing more stress than a century ago—moreover, stress is important! It makes you smarter, faster, and more active, as long as it isn't sustained for too long. The phenomenon of burnout has given rise to a multimillion-dollar industry of self-help to counter its negative effects. Vinkers takes a more skeptical view and believes that simple life lessons like "Spend more time doing nothing" are not very effective. He and the philosopher Jeroen de Ridder wrote that "[self-help] tips, however well-intentioned, are useless: You wouldn't tell a soldier suffering from PTSD to eat more healthily or a single mother in a poor neighborhood to find a hobby." We are all different, living different lives, and we have different responses to stressful problems. There is no ready-made solution. That's why we're drowning in self-help books.

Healthy skepticism isn't a bad thing for your mental health. In the early twentieth century, the Dutch psychiatrist Henricus Cornelius Rümke wrote: "Skepticism can help people develop to their full potential. That doesn't mean you're always beset by insecurity, but that you're aware that reality is complex and there is room to follow your own path in life."

Surely not
EVERYBODY
was
KUNG-FU
FIGHTING!

Stress in the workplace is a vicious cycle. When employees are burned out they slack off in their work, causing their colleagues' workload to increase.

Stress and burnout are a major threat to niksen. If you're emotionally exhausted, you can't stop and do nothing—there's too much going on in your head. The psychologist Thijs Launspach specializes in dealing with stress and burnout and has noticed that more and more companies are taking a preventive approach to tackling pressure at work. Stress in the workplace is a vicious cycle. When employees are burned out they slack off in their work, causing their colleagues' workload to increase. In turn, their colleagues—who may feel a responsibility to step in—become burned out. Launspach has called this a domino effect.

Counterintuitively, Launspach suggests, "A bit of stress is fine: You need it, it makes you perform better." That is, as long as you have strategies to de-stress when you become overwhelmed. There's a big difference between a fast-paced, energetic working environment and one that brings you to tears at the end of every day. If you experience the latter, it's chronic stress—and you need to get a handle on it. According to Launspach, the first step to dealing with stress is recognizing the physical symptoms, which can be different from person to person. A few common ones include headaches, neck or muscle tension, irritability, and forgetfulness. Watch out for these signs, and if they're all too familiar, it's time to take a step back. You can start looking after your body by investing in plenty of sleep, a healthy diet, exercise, and a bit of niksen now and then. If you can't completely switch off for niksen, try reducing the stimuli you're exposed to, switching off your phone, going for walks in nature, or playing. Launspach says, "Those are usually the first things that go out the window as soon as you experience too much stress."

A bit of stress is fine: You need it,
it makes you perform better.

What we really need is a shift in society. Launspach has written about his hope that by 2030 the Netherlands will be a burnout-free country. This will only happen if we break the taboo around stress. "It's time we see people who report stress not as weak but as smart, because they're listening to what their body is telling them," he says, and the first place to start is the workplace. From the top manager to the most junior employee, people need to take care of themselves and look out for each other. Collaborative workplaces are key to fighting burnout, as colleagues can often recognize the warning signs for us much earlier than we can ourselves. Launspach suggests, "It would be great if there was a confidential counselor or a coach or a 'chief happiness officer' who can intervene at an early stage." Having a supportive workplace can do wonders for our mental health. We can stop working crazy hours or eating lunch alone at our desk. Ultimately, we'll be much better employees, and happier people.

BORE-OUT

While niksen can easily slide into brooding or send you back to checking social media, it can also lead to something much worse: Spend too much time doing nothing and you may find yourself with a bore-out. It's the other end of the spectrum from burn-out. While many of us are emotionally exhausted, there are some who feel insufficiently challenged. With too little to do, they are bored to tears. It's a relatively recent phenomenon that has not been researched extensively. It usually involves working below your skill level, and/or not enough hours. It may also result from finishing all your chores and now having absolutely nothing left to do. You may even find that you passed the pleasant stage of boredom long ago and are beginning to lose the will to live. Maybe you're looking for a job but aren't getting anywhere. Or you've had several interviews and are forcing yourself to do a job application a day, but even that's a struggle. Whereas people with burn-out have to avoid stimuli, those with a bore-out should seek them out. You're stressed because you have too little on your plate. It's hard to admit to bore-out, because it makes you sound like a bit of a nerd. Like the kid at school who, just before the bell, reminds the teacher that she hasn't assigned any homework yet.

It's hard to admit to bore-out, because it makes you sound like a bit of a nerd.

ENERGY

You don't need much energy in order to do nothing. When you have a rush of adrenaline you want to keep moving. You're happy and pumped. That's *not* the right moment for niksen. You can't be overexcited, and that's fine; there'll be another time for doing nothing. *The Joy of Laziness* by the German physician Peter Axt and his daughter, Michaela Axt-Gadermann, is a book about *lanterfanten* and physical energy, though the book received little attention in the medical world. They write that all people have a fixed amount of life energy, and we shouldn't use it up all in one go. Their tips: Don't do too much (exercise, but in moderation), sleep a lot, and turn up the heat (or wear your coziest sweaters). It's a terrific book for people who like to mosey through life doing as little as possible and need arguments to persuade their (not very critical) friends. The authors cite the example of animals in captivity generally outliving their counterparts in the wild that are forced to hunt for their food, and the fact that the man who inspired the marathon (Pheidippides, a Greek messenger) died after racing from the town of Marathon to Athens. Regular exercise may help you to live longer, but think about the fact that the time you gain equals the time you put in keeping fit. So perhaps we might as well skip it and stick to "minimal effort." If it sounds too good to be true, it probably is . . .

SITTING

We work too hard and we sit too much. Erik Scherder, a neuropsychologist, encourages people to move as much as possible. In fact, he says the things lazy people would rather not hear: Not only do we sit too much, but sitting is the new smoking. Scherder argues that inactivity, or a lack of exercise, is the fourth leading cause of death worldwide. "A whopping 31 percent of the global population fails to meet the recommended minimum of physical activity. This is up from 17 percent a few years ago; so in three years that figure has nearly doubled. The whole world is sitting down," he said.

People in the Netherlands sit an average of six and a half hours a day, while in the US and UK people average seven hours, with many sitting up to ten hours a day. Many of us sit at work, and spend hours in a chair while scrolling on our phone or computer. Scherder himself owns a desk bike, so he gets a bit of exercise while writing. Inactivity is the root of many health problems, which is why we should really drop the idea of shifting down a gear. We should go for a walk and spend time in nature, which encourages our brains to make new connections. That clashes with the image of niksen as lying apathetically on the couch, digging into more fried chicken, while letting the world and its problems go by. But Scherder and the ideal of niksen *can* live harmoniously side by side! The sweet spot is incorporating more activity between bouts of sitting, not for never taking the weight off your feet again. It's not a case of all-or-nothing: There are times to be active and times for niksen.

"A whopping 31 percent of the global population fails to meet the recommended minimum of physical activity."

THE HEART

After stress in our head and stress in our body, we move on to the heart. A bit of stress is good for you, and the heart knows that. Some kinds of stress keep you alive. Like eustress, which says, "Hey, watch out! A giant seagull wants to steal your ice cream!" Or: "Be careful! That huge truck is going much faster than you think!" This positive form of bodily stress enables you to react and protect your ice cream from that hungry bird and yourself from that speeding vehicle. Genius—thank you, body!

It becomes unhealthy when your body is no longer capable of recovering from that stress, such as when you're squeezing stress balls like crazy and you can't seem to find a moment of calm anywhere. The Centers for Disease Control and Prevention has an online heart age calculator, which computes your risk of cardiovascular disease. The test can be done by any brave soul over the age of forty. Of course, stress in and of itself isn't exactly great for your body, but what makes it even worse is that you often don't take good care of yourself during busy periods. You become wrapped up in other priorities, stuck inside your head, and then neglect your body. You exercise less and eat too much frozen pizza or fast food, or you stop eating all together. Maybe you start drinking and/or smoking more, or you want to get high, to take the edge off things. All that stress can push your heart age higher than your actual years. It may give you palpitations. Suddenly your heart is beating twice as fast as normal, and you fear it might march right out of your body.

It's not always easy to gauge how much stress you're under. For example, some high school students spend an afternoon on their homework—perhaps while watching TikTok and YouTube videos at the same time—and others a full two days. It's not only a question of intelligence but of personality. A super-smart student may have an intense fear of failure and suffer panic attacks while trying to finish the assignment, while another may be more concerned with their parents finding the smoking paraphernalia in their room than with the assignment. And if, as an adult, you have colleagues who are tearing out their hair from stress, you probably feel you should be panicking, too. Then you start worrying and before you know it your brain turns every situation into a dire emergency. And you've dug yourself into a hole: A difference of opinion becomes an ongoing conflict and a setback a major catastrophe.

A bit of stress is good for you, and the heart knows that. Some kinds of stress keep you alive.

A WOMAN'S HEART

For many years, the health of women's hearts received next to no attention because most of the research in this area focused on men. In the 1970s, there was even a study looking at whether wives were making too many demands on their husbands and thus causing their husband's hearts to give out. But in recent years the cardiologist Angela Maas has been at the forefront of efforts to redress this gender bias. She wrote the book *A Woman's Heart* and established a research foundation of the same name. In 2003 she was the first to introduce specialized women's consultations, which led to the discovery that cardiovascular disease presents very differently in women and men. Maas sees the effects of modern life—stress, insufficient rest, information overload, and overcommitment—reflected in heart problems (in both male and female patients). "Our lifestyle is leading to new forms of heart disease. There's an epidemic of cardiac arrhythmias, or atrial fibrillation," she explains. "This used to affect mainly the elderly, but now we're seeing it in younger patients and it's very common. It's associated with obesity and high blood pressure, which can also be stress-related. And we're seeing more and more heart attacks in women aged forty to sixty-five. Not because of clogged arteries, but because of a sudden tear in a blood vessel, a type of heart attack we used to think was quite rare."

"You have to help out with the Christmas decorations and the bake sale, but you still have to go to work, too, and with the roads being busier than ever you end up getting stuck in traffic, and then in the evening you have to go to the gym."

Maas led a study at Tilburg University in the Netherlands that looked into the link between stress and this type of heart attack, called a spontaneous coronary artery dissection (SCAD). The research has not yet been published but has already yielded some interesting results. In a conversation with Maas, she reported finding that this type of heart attack is most prevalent in highly educated women who have few risk factors, such as poor diet and obesity, but who have high levels of stress. These are women who, no doubt, live super-healthy lives. So why the stress? "In the past thirty years the pressure women are under has changed dramatically," suggests Maas. "In the past, many were at home for much of the day, which was perhaps a bit boring and also stressful in

a way, but at least there was enough time to get things done around the house. Today many women work outside the home, and those with children also have all kinds of school-related responsibilities. In other words, there's a lot more to do. My own mother never did anything at my school, even though she was a stay-at-home mom, but these days you're expected to be involved. You have to help out with the Christmas decorations and the bake sale, and you still have to go to work, too, and with the roads being busier than ever you end up getting stuck in traffic, and then in the evening you have to go to the gym." That's a lot—and enough to make your head spin. To make matters worse, many women want to have it all, and do it all. Maas says, "That's a deadly quality. Men are much better at parking stress. They obviously have a lot to do, too, but they're more likely to say: let's call it a day. Women often keep going, both in their work and in their heads. Worry is a big part of perfectionism. You keep going over your to-do lists. Sometimes it helps to write them down, so you don't have to remember everything. We have to learn to park." Balancing it all, you wonder how women who *don't* get heart attacks manage it.

> Many women live by the old adage, which can be applied the world over, "Don't blame, don't complain, but pray for strength."

The other thing you often see in women who have a SCAD is that they experienced burnout the year before, or still have it and haven't made a full recovery yet. Even so, women tend to take on even more commitments and, Maas suggests, are partly responsible for their own burnouts. "That's not a popular thing to say, but it's true. When you have too much going on and you're living in a pressure cooker, you can suddenly have this type of heart attack. It always happens at an otherwise perfectly calm moment. A woman may be having a cup of tea one evening and then bam!" One of the tell-tale signs is an extreme kind of fatigue, something you've never experienced before. "Out of the blue you feel too tired to climb the stairs or you have to stop to catch your breath. There's this sudden decline in your fitness. When you notice that, it's bound to be something serious. It can be anemia, but it's best to get such a serious dip in fitness checked out," she says. And we haven't even mentioned menopause yet, which comes with its own set of stresses. Maas would like to see women talk more openly about the problems they experience during menopause. Many women live by the old adage, which can be applied the world over, "Don't blame, don't complain, but pray for strength." Menopause can be dramatic: Imagine you're in a meeting and suddenly you feel as if someone is aiming a blowtorch at you; you're sweating profusely and can no longer think straight. You're trying to string a sentence together, but the only thought that forms involves ice cubes and ice skating in a bikini. In such a situation—which is not all that uncommon—you should be able to say to your colleagues, "I'm taking a short break to cool down and I'll be back when my body temperature has dipped below boiling point again." But instead, women keep working away, pretending that their hormones are not all over the place. And the same is true for menstruation. Maas recommends that women ask to work from home more often.

The drawback of doing nothing is that it doesn't burn a lot of calories.

Let's go back to niksen—the extreme version. Many people don't get enough exercise. Isn't that a problem, too? "Absolutely. It's often a vicious circle. Sometimes you meet a woman over fifty and you wonder: What happened? She's gained thirty pounds in a year and has hit rock bottom. Everything aches: joints, knees, hips. You can recommend more exercise, but that's not an option at that point. Postmenopausal women often find themselves in a tight spot that's hard to get out of. Doctors tend to put all of these women who are over fifty on antidepressants. I'm exaggerating, but I do see it a lot. What we need is more openness and understanding." In practice that means that we need to talk about our ailments more. Complain, women, complain! Get help when you can't handle it anymore, but don't overdo it. That's never a good idea, and especially not when it comes to niksen. Before you know it, you have one hundred pounds to shed, and that's hard for anyone, not just menopausal or postmenopausal women. Plenty of studies have shown that being completely lazy and never exercising—full-time niksen—will only wreak more havoc. The drawback of doing nothing is that it doesn't burn a lot of calories, so you'll have to cut back on what you eat. Maybe a light salad and a sandwich, but if you do nothing and still devour bags of chips and french fries, those arteries are going to clog up, and that's bad for your heart. It's true that women need to slow down (more than men!), but stopping completely won't be good for anyone.

SLOWLY DOES IT

In recent decades, the type of work we do in society has radically changed. A century ago, most of us were toiling away in the fields; now, many people sit staring at small screens all day. The boundary between work and private life is blurring and few have the ambition to report to the same boss for thirty years. It certainly explains the growing interest in slow living, in taking a timeout and a step back, in thinking about what really matters in life. We're going back to the basics. This has taken on many trendy forms: yoga, holism, mindfulness—you name it. You can try sensory deprivation therapy, watch autonomous sensory meridian response (ASMR) videos, do some mindful gardening, or go on a silent retreat in an old monastery in Italy. Anything to get some peace of mind so we can cope with our hectic lives again. We'll keep saying it: Doing nothing is hard. It's tempting to reach for your phone, a crossword puzzle, a newspaper, just to be doing something. You're looking for distraction, for entertainment, and it's available in spades. Take the thousands of notifications that pop up on your phone. The result is a never-ending stream of stimulation that stops us from seeing the forest for the trees.

You can try sensory deprivation therapy, watch autonomous sensory meridian response (ASMR) videos, do some mindful gardening, or go on a silent retreat in an old monastery in Italy.

Many of us are looking for ways to calm down and insulate ourselves from these stimuli. A frequently tried method is mindfulness. It fits right in with the "slow living" trend and encourages us to go about our lives more

deliberately, and switch off autopilot. That way you don't find yourself at the checkout paying for one hundred dollars' worth of groceries without remembering how any of them ended up in your cart. Don't chomp your way through a dozen cookies, but savor one or two and really take your time. By giving attention to everything you do you create more time for what really matters in life. You try to rein in your wandering thoughts: *No, stop thinking about how cute puppies are and what a shame it is they're so demanding. Back to reading this book. Not as in, "I'll read for another half hour and then I'll do the vacuuming."* Instead, focus on the fact that you're reading and that's all you're doing right now. This and nothing else. In the present moment.

By giving attention to everything you do you create more time for what really matters in life.

One of the people who introduced Buddhist teaching to the West under the term *mindfulness* is Jon Kabat-Zinn. Originally a molecular biologist, he developed an interest in Eastern philosophy in the 1960s and studied with the Zen master Seung Sahn. Together with the Vietnamese Zen Buddhist Thich Nhat Hanh he created mindfulness-based stress reduction (MBSR), an eight-week training program combining yoga and meditation. Kabat-Zinn himself takes a fairly relaxed approach to his teachings. There are no strict rules. A few years ago, in response to a question about the main takeaway from mindfulness, he told the Dutch magazine *Happinez* that for him it was the realization that we shouldn't take things too personally.

> When something happens to us, we take it personally. Someone puts us on a pedestal and we think, you see, I'm awesome. But then someone else comes along who picks out our mistakes and we think we're awful. But in

> actual fact we're neither; not a saint and not a sinner. You are who you are and things happen. If you make everything about you, you end up hurting yourself sooner or later and there's no need for that.

We can take the same approach to niksen. Thoughts come and go. We don't have to take them all equally seriously. Sometimes it's okay to simply let them be.

Mindfulness can be amazing, but it requires effort. Some people claim you might as well go bowling, because it's just as effective as mindfully raking up leaves in the garden. But mindfulness practitioners don't care, because with a bit of luck they've already let go of their ego and don't take those views personally.

Mindfulness is to niksen as Kate Middleton is to Meghan Markle. Here's how. Having survived the many years of mudslinging by the British tabloid press, Kate is now proudly doing the royal wave as the future queen of the United Kingdom. Meghan, meanwhile, stuck it out for a year before doing a runner and going her own way. Kate has a higher purpose and is extremely disciplined. Meghan has no staying power and does her own thing. Surely this analogy is crystal-clear and in no way flawed. In all seriousness, mindfulness also has a higher purpose: It's about becoming the queen of your own life. It's about learning to ride this crazy highway of life, making sense of it, and putting it into perspective. Niksen is none of these things. It's not an approach, it's not a solution to anything. It's too small and insignificant for that. As soon as it becomes more than insignificant, it's no longer niksen. You're not meant to take time for it—except at the beginning, to actually make it happen. Ultimately, you should just slip into doing nothing without being aware of it. It's not until you're about to fall over with hunger that you realize, *Hey, I was completely absent for a while and it was wonderful.*

HYPERSENSITIVITY

If you find it harder than most to deal with sensory overload you may be a highly sensitive person (HSP): someone with a heightened response to sensory stimuli. Elke van Hoof, a clinical psychologist who wrote a book on the subject, says that an estimated 15 percent of all Dutch people are HSP. The same goes for people around the world. She describes the phenomenon as follows:

> The defining aspect of hypersensitivity is the way an HSP processes sensory information. Because of this heightened response to stimuli, HSPs experience the world around them in a fundamentally different way compared to non-HSPs. Someone who is highly sensitive is very skilled at both observing and thoroughly processing external factors. As a consequence, they are particularly susceptible to overstimulation and intense emotions.

Though HSPs will find it harder than the rest of us to practice niksen, they need it most to stave off overstimulation.

MEDITATION

A key component of mindfulness is meditation. It's a way of focusing the mind and achieving calm. Many religions know some form of meditation, reflection, or contemplation. When the Buddha himself felt empty inside he decided to withdraw. The idea behind meditation is to get to know your own mind better. For example, when you're irritable because someone said something stupid to you, and you focus on your breathing—and only on your breathing—you're actually meditating and you'll automatically grow calmer. As the Dalai Lama puts it, you're listening to your emotions, while at the same time letting them go. You don't meditate with the aim of reaching nirvana but because you want to be able to deal with the ebb and flow of daily emotions. There are many different types of meditation. A few minutes a day can make a huge difference. You don't have to spend years in a cave in complete isolation like a Tibetan monk or Saint Francis of Assisi, because there's no such thing as a higher degree in meditation. It's not a rigidly defined practice, and the best thing about it is that you can't be good or bad at it. It's just something you do.

Meditation is not a rigidly defined practice, and the best thing about it is that you can't be good or bad at it.

Those who want to take it a step further can try transcendental meditation (TM). This is the brainchild of Maharishi Mahesh Yogi, who was famously the Beatles's guru. He turned meditation into a global phenomenon. The film director David Lynch is another well-known fan of transcendental meditation. He had a lot of anger, he recounted in a documentary for the History Channel in 2007, but within two weeks of meditating it all "lifted away." When you learn transcendental meditation you're given a personal mantra, which, when you know how to use it properly, will yield the maximum benefit.

Meditation has been described and practiced by spiritual leaders and religions the world over. It has a very long history, but the common denominator is the quest for peaceful silence within ourselves. Eckhart Tolle, one of the most popular spiritual teachers today, describes meditation as simply being wholly present in the moment, without adding any thoughts to the mix. That could mean sitting on the couch in your onesie, watching the cat playing with a toy mouse. Or listening to the sound of the dishwasher, or a lawn mower somewhere in the distance. The challenge lies in not letting your thoughts wander to the meal that has to be cooked, or to any other future plans or past problems. Thoughts pop into your head all the time and all for free, but you have to let them pass in this moment. Live in the now—which happens to be the title of the book that made his name: *The Power of Now*.

Eckhart Tolle, one of the most popular spiritual teachers today, describes mediation as simply being wholly present in the moment, without adding any thoughts to the mix.

A LESSON FROM THE ANIMAL KINGDOM

We have an important lesson to learn from our fellow creatures in the animal kingdom. Cats lie down for much of the day. Lions are big cats and also sleep a lot (they can mate up to fifty times a day, but always very briefly). Animals have the advantage of living outside, and they don't have rent or a mortgage to pay. Their food is free, but they do have to forage for it (at least those that live in the wild do). Reproducing and not dying—these are their main challenges. The lesson? Live in the moment. At most, they plan a few minutes ahead, when they're about to catch an antelope, but otherwise they instinctively do as they please.

MEDITATION AND SCIENCE

There's some scientific evidence for the benefits of meditation in recent studies. For a long time, science didn't consider meditation; studies tended to focus on people's psychological problems and less on the effects of the more spiritual ways of dealing with them. But this is changing. In 2017 Daniel Goleman, a science journalist, and Richard Davidson, a research professor of psychology and psychiatry, published a book about these studies, called *Altered Traits: Science Reveals How Meditation Changes Your Mind, Brain, and Body*. Davidson did his own research with the French Buddhist monk Matthieu Ricard, who helped convince monks living deep in the Himalayas to take part in the study. The results of their brain scans were astonishing: The monks were found to have much-stronger-than-average gamma waves, even during sleep, which suggests that meditation has a lasting effect. Gamma waves are involved in higher cognitive processes—more precisely, in establishing connections. Meditation was shown to have an anti-aging effect on the brain and to alter the experience of pain. But let's not forget that we're talking about monks, who, as the scientists say, have extensive meditation experience. All of which is to say, there's still a lot we don't know. There is no doubt that scientists are doing great work, but there are many factors to consider. What if all the participants were on a strict diet? Or maybe they were all born with greater gamma wave activity, which is why they started meditating in the first place? For every study claiming that a glass of red wine with dinner is really healthy there are a dozen that contradict it. It's like reading the bible.

It's not just for hippies in caftans who are stuck in the sixties.

Research suggests that meditation does have an effect: It has been shown to alter our gray matter. This came out of a study among sixteen volunteers who were new to the practice and meditated thirty minutes a day for eight weeks. Years later, a study at Harvard found evidence of more gray matter in various parts of the brain in those who meditate. Sara Lazar, the neuroscientist who led the study, is a meditation aficionado herself. A few years ago, after a personal crisis, the Flemish neurologist Steven Laureys took up the practice. An immediate convert, he was determined to find a scientific underpinning. He describes it as a workout for the brain, comparable to what sports does for the body. But he acknowledges that the effects are difficult to quantify. It's one thing to examine Buddhist monks who have been meditating their whole lives, but there is no way of knowing what their brains would have looked like had they not spent all this time practicing. In other words, it's hard to corroborate the findings. But Laureys is keen to share his enthusiasm. He stresses that meditation is not some weird alternative practice: It's not just for hippies in caftans who are stuck in the sixties. Anybody can try it and—who knows?—benefit from it.

PRACTICAL TIPS:

How to relax

"**You have to be** very strong in yourself for niksen," explains Miriam Evers of Slowww, a Dutch online community for women. Through training sessions, yoga, and retreats she tries to help people to relax. "The world is full of distractions—from our phones to TV series to evening classes. It's very tempting to keep busy." So how can we relax? Here are some tips from Evers.

Minimize.

People often feel that if they want to relax, they need to spring into action—set their alarm and start the day by meditating for half an hour. There's no need to introduce such big changes. Small changes are easier and can act as a catalyst. The moment you begin to relax, it becomes easier to look at your life from a distance, and you're less likely to feel compelled to do or buy something or fill that emptiness in another way. Begin by lying down for five minutes. You can close your eyes, but you don't have to. All you need to do is create a bit of space to process all the stimuli, and then the agitation will ease. Link moments of relaxation to one or more daily routines, like waiting for the subway or making a cup of tea.

Check in every once in a while.

When you're reading a book or watching TV, you may be relaxing, but you're also checking out. You're placing your attention outside of yourself. It's important to regularly check in with yourself, and you can really only do this at moments when you're not focusing on external things. When you turn inward you feel how you're really feeling. It's something I see in yoga. When people lie down in a particular pose for five minutes, even if it's not very demanding physically, it really knocks them sideways after a hectic day. They feel restless; they're not used to doing nothing.

Do one thing at a time.

When you have children clamoring for attention, it may be tempting to play a game while checking your phone at the same time. Try to keep your attention firmly on one thing. Children know when you're trying to do several things at once. Those of you without kids hanging on your legs are surely guilty of multitasking, too. Try doing just one thing, and be amazed at your focus.

Relax in public.

This one is for employees. I often notice that people struggle to do relaxation exercises in public. So if you want to do a breathing exercise you could go somewhere private, like a restroom. It also helps to turn to a colleague who may want to do the same. Not only is it easier to practice together, but you can joke about it and make it all a bit more lighthearted.

TIPS

- **Start small. Introduce mini-moments when you don't do anything, or perhaps only a few breathing exercises.**
- **Be mindful of the difference between checking out and checking in.**
- **Do one thing at a time.**
- **Turn to a colleague so you can build in moments of rest together.**

SITTING HERE
BY THE WINDOW
feeling bored as ever
I WISH I WAS
TWO TINY DOGS
so I could play together

"Spleen" by Michel van der Plas
(translated from the Dutch)

3

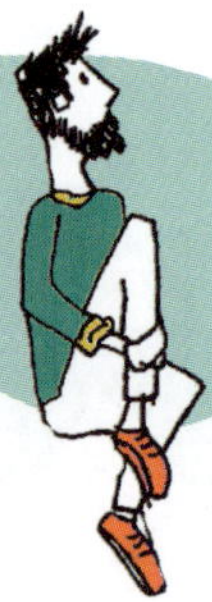

Niksen and the outside world

TOPICS

- **Daydreaming in the Middle Ages**
- **The advent of machines**
- **The attention economy**
- **The poetry of procrastination**

W**e've been trying** to enjoy doing nothing for centuries, but we keep getting distracted. Initially it was by hunger, disease, and war, later by financial crises and social unrest. Niksen doesn't move mountains, ease traffic congestion, or contribute to a pension fund. It's not tax-deductible either. In short, it seems to have no practical purpose. Besides, indolence gives you too much time to think, which makes you morose or, worse, rebellious. The average Dutch person prefers to work. Work takes your mind off things and has evident value. It's no wonder we've turned away from leisure, but how did we end up in this position? Put differently: How come we still haven't figured out how to achieve work–life balance?

Life in today's ADHD-addled society appears to be just as stressful as it was in the Middle

Ages. The Netherlands is often described as a country with a Calvinist mindset: Work, don't whine. But we possessed a strong work ethic long before the Reformation, fueled in part by the belief that, expelled from Paradise, we were forced to work for our supper. By the time Calvin appeared on the scene, in the sixteenth century, humanity had been working hard and discovering the world for quite a while.

The Netherlands is often described as a country with a Calvinist mindset: Work, don't whine.

Look at the Netherlands and what do you see? The chances are you're seeing a neat and tidy country. There are hardly any old buildings that have been derelict for years or scrubby woodland that no one even knows exists. Everything has been mapped; everything has a plan and a purpose. One reason for this is the fact that we live below sea level, and that's hard work. It's arduous to build dikes to stop the country from flooding—and that same water is used for trade, taking us away from our shores, to sell our exports around the globe.

SAYINGS

Dutch proverbs praising industry and thrift show that historically the Netherlands and niksen are not a great match. We're a mercantile people, first and foremost, which brings us in contact with the outside world. Time and your inner world may already be cared for, but before you can start doing nothing you'll need to get the rest of society on board. As the Dutch say:

- Better to lose your labor than your time in idleness.
- A plow that works shines, but standing water stinks.
- When hard work goes out the door, poverty comes in the window.

THE LAND OF COCKAIGNE

The Dutch never learned to sit still. Herman Pleij, professor emeritus of medieval literature at the University of Amsterdam, says, "The Dutch tend to pride themselves on their Calvinist mind-set, and that means toiling away. But this is just a construct, part of our settlement history. It's not in our genes, or in our DNA. You may hear people say that it is, but it's not true. We're merchants. And the idea that our tendency to keep busy has Calvinist origins is nonsense, too, because this mercantile mentality arose much earlier in the Low Countries."

In the Middle Ages life was hard for everyone, whether you were a peasant or a wealthy landowner. Movies about knights make it look like great fun, but life was incredibly tough. You could be married off at the age of twelve! Winters were often freezing cold, with subzero temperatures for weeks on end. The cold also meant there was less food. If you were lucky enough to survive the winter, you might be struck down by one of the epidemics that often followed the wintry chill. As if these circumstances weren't harsh enough, there was the constant fear of ending up in hell after you died.

Our medieval ancestors liked distraction as much as anyone, and so they daydreamed about a mythical country where food was plentiful and you didn't have to work: Cockaigne. It is a magical land where people lived like the brothers and sisters of kings (with all the advantages but none of the responsibilities that come with royalty). The 1567 painting *The Land of Cockaigne* by Pieter Bruegel the Elder shows three men reclining beside a tree, resting after a heavy meal, while a bird lies on a platter before them, ready to be eaten. A piglet wanders around with a knife already inserted into its belly. Cockaigne is clearly not populated by vegetarians. Everyone is unemployed, as work is forbidden. In this land you could spend all day eating yourself silly and doing nothing and it wouldn't cost you a penny. And since there are no possessions, there is no envy either. It is a land with rivers of wine and an abundance of roast chicken and turkey. Everyone is up for sex and—particularly important to the Dutch—the weather is always stable and mild.

Herman Pleij wrote a book about this never-never land, *Dreaming of Cockaigne: Medieval Fantasies of the Perfect Life*, in which he writes:

> In the Middle Ages, too, there were times when people were bored out of their mind and had to make their own entertainment. When the weather was bad, for instance, or after heavy rain, the roads were impassable and people were forced to remain indoors. When you finally had a visitor, perhaps a mendicant monk who'd schlepped through the mud, you were desperate for stories. So the poor man would invent the craziest knights' tales, and these are our sources now.

In the sixteenth century, the British humanist Thomas More introduced the term *Utopia*, but that was nothing like Cockaigne. Pleij says, "More's utopia was social critique, satire. Cockaigne, which came to be called Luilekkerland around that time, was anything but." In Dutch, *Luilekkerland* literally translates as "lazyluscIousland"—every person's dream.

> It served to distract and allay fears of not having enough to eat. The fear of famine was even felt by wealthier citizens. Life was changeable and frost instantly led to major problems, followed shortly after by disease. This precarious balance created the need for compensation and jokes so you could laugh at your own suffering, and that's what Cockaigne was all about. These fantasies . . . reflected the concerns of society at that time.

LIFE

IS NOT A

succession

of BREATHTAKING

MOMENTS

THAT

sounds more

like ASTHMA...

Sloth was one of the seven capital sins, and in medieval times the concept broadened to encompass laziness. Prints of Bruegel's *The Land of Cockaigne* were captioned: "Sticking your hands under your armpits is the devil's work."

Cockaigne was an escape from the idea disseminated by the Church that work was God's punishment for man because Adam and Eve had flouted his rules in Paradise. Pleij suggests, "In the Middle Ages, people believed there was still a paradise somewhere, but that it was closed to them." This is a reasonable coping mechanism when surrounded by so much fear and hunger. They loved to daydream about that paradise—and still do. "Normal people ate twice a day; monks and nuns only once," says Pleij. "You were gluttonous if you ate three meals, or all day long. In large cities today you can eat day and night, and that's a relatively recent phenomenon." The irony is that those dreams of gluttony have become reality in modern society.

Sloth was one of the seven capital sins, and in medieval times the concept broadened to encompass laziness. Prints of Bruegel's *The Land of Cockaigne* were captioned: "Sticking your hands under your armpits is the devil's work." If you stopped working you'd start brooding, become melancholic, and eventually crave death. And that was the work of the devil. We live in the land of Cockaigne now and yet we're still in search of happiness: How is that possible? Pleij suggests, "It's never enough. The one constant in this story, throughout the ages, is people trying to get a handle on things, direct their lives, and gain control. People will never stop trying."

THE INDUSTRIAL REVOLUTION

In the Middle Ages people dreamed about doing nothing and haven't stopped since. We all desperately want to indulge in niksen, but unlike hard work—which is encouraged in society—niksen rarely gets the praise it deserves. By the Industrial Revolution our desires hadn't changed, nor had our situation improved. Making money became a very real possibility for more and more people and marked the start of the rat race. If you worked hard, you could grow rich. A certain ambivalence about leisure time remained into the twentieth century, but there were always people who tried to make us see the benefits of *lanterfanten*. In 1951, a local Dutch newspaper published an article encouraging its readers to sit beside a splendid orchid in bloom and do nothing for an hour or so. "Some people are so caught up in the hustle and bustle of city life, they can no longer sit still. And yet it's the best way to vacation."

Unlike hard work—which is encouraged in society—niksen rarely gets the praise it deserves.

THE WORKWEEK

In centuries past, the Dutch didn't work a carefully timed forty hours a week, but double or even triple that. In 1919, the Netherlands welcomed the Labor Act, which stipulated that all employees were entitled to one day off every week. Thanks to the influence of Christian parties, this became Sunday, so everyone could attend church. Saturday eventually became a half day. After World War II, men had to work a bit longer again to get the economy back on track; the minimum at the time was forty-eight hours a week. With increased prosperity came another reduction in work hours, and in the 1960s employers began to experiment with five-day workweeks. The European Union has now capped a workweek at forty-eight hours, but the average in the Netherlands is thirty-six to thirty-eight hours. Meanwhile, in the US, the Fair Labor Standards Act of 1940 officially limited the workweek to forty hours, though it's common for people to log many more.

From the passing of the Labor Act on, Dutch people were officially entitled to time for themselves and, enterprising as we are, instantly built an entire leisure industry around it. Since it wasn't seen in a positive light, niksen wasn't on the agenda. You can sleep when you're dead. It makes you miserable, and for the believers there was the added complication that doing nothing is an obstacle on the path to heaven. For Catholics, idleness (sloth) is a capital sin. And even the liberals say that work gives meaning to life. Has there ever been a time when the whole country could sit on its backside and take it easy?

FEMINISM

Over the years, time spent on household chores has fallen. Women are especially likely to think to themselves: *Why iron these sheets when a) nobody notices, and b) everything's all crumpled again in the morning?* As washing machines, vacuum cleaners, and blenders gave women more time, the advent of air-conditioned offices, sedentary work, and regulations surrounding working hours and weekends off meant that the time was ripe for them to start exploring the labor market. Slowly, of course, with baby steps. Those who opted to stay at home encountered a new phenomenon: leisure time.

In 1952, the children's book author Eline Capit won a prize for her detective story *Run from the Sheep*. She had written it "in the wee hours, when [her] daughters were asleep." She followed it with a few more thrillers, as well as a column in a Dutch daily newspaper about the ups and downs of life in her household. Among other things, she wrote about the nanny she hired for her children, the hurdles to having a telephone installed at home, and about motherhood being a job "that rarely comes with a severance package." In 1964 she wrote a column highlighting the benefits of neglecting housework, of just not bothering every now and then. She had no domestic help, and the house was far too big to keep spotless, so she let things slide.

Niksen is a feminist act of resistance.

In the piece Capit highlights the advantages of a filthy house: no more visitors or, as she puts it, no more "inspections." She writes, "If I want to be rid of guests altogether, all I have to do is show them the

cabinet under the sink where an old sponge sits with a bunch of ancient cleaning rags, which have become a funky-smelling basket." It may be a mess inside the Capit family home, but she relishes her time for doing nothing. Niksen is a feminist act of resistance. Three cheers for Eline Capit! A few months later, she received the backing of the magazine *Libelle* as they took a tentative step toward women's liberation. In January 1965 *Libelle* floated an audacious idea—that women should claim more time for themselves. Even so, the editorial board was apprehensive about broaching this subject and hedged with readers, writing: "Will you please do your best to understand?" It's hard to imagine now that only fifty-five years ago the subject of carving out more time for oneself had to be treated with kid gloves, but *Libelle* was extremely circumspect when addressing its readers, who were mainly housewives. "You see, it's your leisure time we're talking about. No, no, please don't say you don't have any. You're awfully busy. You work from dawn until dusk and then you collapse onto your bed and sleep like a log." The women's magazine went on to ask its readers: "But be honest, could you not contrive to take a bit of time for yourself each week?" *Libelle* cautiously suggested encouraging the husband to spend an evening with the children. "Maybe he'll roar with laughter when you propose it to him, but surely he will recognize that your request is entirely reasonable!" The housewife wasn't supposed to fill this time with selfish naps or aimless strolls, but with sewing, cooking, or upholstery classes. "Who knows how much more enjoyable housekeeping will be once you know a bit more about the individual components, and earn the admiration of your entire social circle." *Libelle* saw a trend emerging: "All over the country, overstretched housewives are taking a few hours off every week to escape the drudgery."

With the feminist movement, we acquired more leisure time—and in the 1950s, television entered our living rooms. Before then, people had been glued to the radio from time to time, but this new technology really made people put their feet up. After a hard day's work the TV was turned on and never really switched off again. While TV has taken on a new form with the arrival of the internet, we're still binge-watching series.

Libelle cautiously suggested encouraging the husband to spend an evening with the children.

HIP

Since the start of the twenty-first century, niksen and lanterfanten have been all the rage. The Dutch have created *chillen*, their own take on the English "chilling." At the turn of the millennium the Dutch were really into lounging: They had lounge cafés where people arranged weary limbs on couches, ordered something to drink, and daydreamed about partying on Ibiza to unwind. In 2001 the Dutch linguistics magazine *Onze Taal* asked its readers to come up with Dutch alternatives for the verb "to lounge," and some of them proposed "niksen," but according to the editors, lounging is so much more than niksen, and they're right, of course. It requires an array of cushions and a groovy slow beat. For niksen you need—you've guessed it—absolutely nothing. Only the courage, the inclination, and the time to clear your head and stare into space.

WALLET

These days we have a fair amount of leisure time at our disposal, as well as the money to do something fun. For many years, money was a big obstacle to doing nothing. In fact, people with mortgages are still scared to slam on the brakes, but there is hope. There is talk among economists of systems that revolve not around growth but around maintaining the status quo. Some people are choosing to hang up their corporate suits in favor of a more minimalist lifestyle. Material possessions are losing their appeal, and the sharing economy is on the rise. Whether you want to work long hours with the aim of growing richer or happier, or you want to enjoy the status quo, niksen is inclusive and available to all. And this is where that Dutch mercantile mentality comes in again, because let's not forget the big benefit of niksen: It's free! You don't need anything for it and you can do it anytime and anywhere. You don't have to invest extra in food, either, because all this hanging around doesn't consume much energy. You can even do it with friends. It's a no-brainer: Niksen can save you a bundle of cash—not least because you're doing nothing instead of something that costs money. If you commit to niksen for, say, an hour or longer, you're not going online to shop for new clothes or unnecessary gadgets. You're not replacing something that doesn't need replacing. You're saving money because you're not spending it on things you don't actually need. Once you start doing nothing, you'll change the way you organize your finances.

Let's not forget the big benefit of niksen:
It's free! You don't need anything for it and you
can do it anytime and anywhere.

MONEY FOR NOTHING

Earning money by doing nothing is a dream for many. If only you were the heir to a multimillion-dollar empire, even one with a dodgy reputation or in the throes of a power struggle. Or how about winning the lottery? Behind their computers, office workers daydream of hammocks on unspoiled beaches under a hot, tropical sun. It's not quite the same if you have to use up all your savings to spend two weeks pretending to be rich. So why not allow yourself to get carried away by the dream lives of people who've managed to amass such wealth that they can afford to spend the rest of their lives doing nothing?

1. **HEIRS:** Rich heirs like Paris Hilton don't have to work a single day of their lives. Paris was pretty much the original influencer: She was the first to earn big money from her status as an "it girl," or socialite. Without a career to speak of, she became famous for who she was—a party animal who liked to flash the cash—and managed to develop that image into an empire. People dismissed her as stupid, like they did with Kylie Jenner, but both young women have built entire brands around their personalities. They cultivated the rich life to become even richer. And that's pretty smart, actually. It made Jenner the youngest-ever self-made billionaire.
2. **LOTTERY WINNERS:** It's hard to think of an easier road to riches: buying a ticket and winning big. That said, few lottery winners stop working altogether; at most they work a bit less. A Swedish study found that lottery winners are definitely happier than non-winners. The money plays a role in this, as does the feeling of being a winner. That effect can last up to twenty years.
3. **THE MAN WHO OUTSOURCED HIS JOB TO CHINA:** "Bob," an unremarkable computer programmer, had been employed by Verizon for many years until it emerged that he wasn't doing the work himself. He had been paying a Chinese company a fifth of his salary to do his job for him while he spent his time surfing the web.

FLEXTIME

The Netherlands is a global leader in part-time employment. Around half of all working people in the country work part time. That's 4.4 million people. Over the years, the concept of "full time" has been subject to deflation, but perhaps its definitive end is now in sight. More and more studies suggest that shorter workdays equal higher productivity. And working from home, which saves travel time, is on the rise, too. Given that time is a major condition for doing nothing, more of it could give niksen a big boost.

If you have an office-based job, you may have heard of "The New World of Work." In 2005, Bill Gates released a memo by that name in which he talked about new technologies changing the way we work. He predicted a trend in people sharing their workspaces and a significant increase in personal productivity. He opened the doors to more flexible workplaces and working hours. It not only saves on overhead but also keeps young people, who cherish their freedom, happy for longer.

WORKING FEWER HOURS

In his book *The 4-Hour Workweek*, Timothy Ferriss claims that an entire workweek can fit into just a few hours if you do your best and learn how to outsource. Unfortunately, it hasn't been embraced by the whole of society yet, not least because some people work in client-facing roles that are difficult to do remotely. In the Netherlands, the thirty-six-hour workweek is pretty much the standard. The rest of our hours are personal time, which includes things like showering, sleeping, and watching TV. Every year, the Netherlands Institute for Social Research investigates our well-being. In a 2016 study they found that men and women both have around forty-three to forty-four hours of free time each week at their disposal, but women spend more time on "personal grooming." Here are some more interesting findings.

- Three quarters of those surveyed want to work on "personal development" in their free time.
- For years we've been very happy with the amount of free time we have (70 percent say it's enough).
- An overwhelming majority likes to unwind during their free time (over 90 percent).
- Most people like to live a quiet life but feel their lives are too busy.
- Interviews and focus groups suggest that women feel greater responsibility for the household and childcare and that they dedicate some of their free time to this.
- Women find it harder to relax.

BULLSHIT JOBS

Alongside shorter workdays and flexible working hours that perhaps better suit our circadian rhythm, even more revolutionary ideas about how we think about work have been proposed. Faster lines of communication and greater flexibility have brought a lot of change, too, but there is still some way to go. The anthropologist David Graeber believes that having a job is outdated. In the past, people worked to produce things, but these days few employees actually manufacture something tangible. Many people work around these products, sometimes at such a great distance that they no longer understand how little a cog they are in the overall machine. Graeber, an activist who played a key role in the Occupy Wall Street movement, describes these roles as "bullshit jobs." After extensive research he came to the conclusion that 20 percent of Western working people believe their job is pointless. There are the paper pushers, for instance, or people who are no longer needed but who can't be fired. Bullshit. Or the personal assistants to bosses who are ignored by the executives and who effectively no longer have a role in the company, but keep up the illusion that what they do matters. And then there are those who work in a coordinating or managing role that often makes them wonder, *What exactly am I doing here?*

After extensive research, David Graeber came to the conclusion that 20 percent of Western working people believe their job is pointless.

Economists have been predicting for some time that the advance of technology will enable people to work less. In the twentieth century, the influential thinker John Maynard Keynes predicted workweeks of just a few hours. This is still far from reality, possibly because he hadn't foreseen all the extra labor needed to produce the internet, game consoles, and airplanes. Graeber disagrees, as only a handful of people are involved in the manufacturing of these. After being designed, they're pulled together by machines; it's all done in a flash. The real problem, in his view, is that many people have unnecessary jobs. So, you have a job that you feel is pointless, but it pays the bills and gives you social standing, because people think you have gainful employment.

GRAEBER'S FIVE TYPES OF BS JOBS (FROM *BULLSHIT JOBS: A THEORY*)

1. **FLUNKIES**: "Flunky jobs are those that exist only or primarily to make someone else look or feel important." An example is a personal assistant with little to do but research skiing trips and forward emails. The sole reason for this function is to show others that someone who has a PA must be a VIP.
2. **GOONS:** Graeber uses an analogy that "countries need armies only because other countries have armies." These are jobs that wouldn't exist if all companies agreed to stop using them, like telemarketers or corporate lawyers.
3. **DUCT TAPERS**: "Duct tapers are employees whose jobs exist only because of a glitch or fault in the organization; who are there to solve a problem that ought not to exist." He compares their activities to putting a bucket underneath a leaking roof and emptying it every half hour instead of calling in a plumber to fix the problem once and for all.
4. **BOX TICKERS**: "I am using the term 'box tickers' to refer to employees who exist only or primarily to allow an organization to be able to claim it is doing something that, in fact, it is not doing." This is common in many public sector jobs, according to Graeber, but businesses are guilty of it, too.
5. **TASKMASTERS:** These are the people whose job it is to assign work to others: "unnecessary superiors, or middle management." He describes the case of a man hired by a bank to streamline workflows, but who never actually saw any of his proposals implemented because they all ended up in the trash. For example, when he suggested that a flunky be fired, he was met with opposition because this worker was important to another manager's ego.

Now then, none of this shows the workplace at its best, and perhaps many of you can relate to it. BS jobs create dissatisfaction, as well as the bore-outs mentioned earlier. Graeber argues for a universal basic income (UBI), which is effectively a pension for all: a minimum monthly income you can live on and which you're free to supplement by working as much as you like. The money in question—say a thousand dollars a month—would be paid into your account, whether you're a billionaire or not. It would eradicate poverty and lead to economic equality.

The American anthropologist David Graeber believes that having a job is outdated. In the past, people worked to produce things, but these days few people actually manufacture something tangible.

The idea of a UBI has been floating around for many years in the Netherlands, too, but it's a huge operation and more research is needed. It calls for a complete overhaul of the current system, and the way we look at work will have to change drastically.

THE ATTENTION ECONOMY

We may all think we'll have more free time in the future. Then the big question remains: What are we going to do with it? There are tons of new products fighting for our attention and companies making the most ingenious devices that offer endless distraction. It's a billion-dollar industry. Some experts believe we live in an "attention economy" in which our lives ultimately revolve around sales. The behavioral scientist Nir Eyal, author of *Hooked: How to Build Habit-Forming Products*, examines how people can be made even more addicted. To clarify, he's not saying that it's a shame we're all glued to our phones. No, his message is about the ability of design to increase engagement—not to make money. It worked. His book became a bestseller and was widely read in the business community.

The battle for our attention has transformed the entertainment industry, too, with consumers now having access to a deluge of films and series on a multitude of platforms. When Martin Scorsese released his gangster movie *The Irishman* on Netflix, he urged his fans not to watch it on their phones. You don't even have to go to the cinema to see the latest film of the renowned, Oscar-winning filmmaker. Scorsese was worried that a small screen wouldn't show his work to its best advantage, which is understandable. When you're watching *The Irishman* on a train, for example, you can be distracted by the conductor, a couple making out in your eyeline, or by a smell you can't place.

With all these companies investing in attracting and retaining your attention, it's hard not to give in and watch a new series each week while simultaneously playing games on your phone. Luckily, five years after

Hooked, Eyal published *Indistractable: How to Control Your Attention and Choose Your Life*, in which he explains how you can overcome your addictions. He knows how we get hooked—and so also knows how we can wean ourselves off this drug. It's difficult, though, not least because our phones are also a handy tool for making better use of our time.

When you're watching *The Irishman* on a train you can be distracted by the conductor, a couple making out in your eyeline, or by a smell you can't place.

HOW TO SOUND IMPORTANT

The made-up Dutch word *epibreren* was introduced in 1954 by the author Simon Carmiggelt. Although totally meaningless, you can use it to make those around you believe you're doing something incredibly worthwhile (when in actual fact you're planning to do nada). Carmiggelt claims it was first coined by a civil servant. You'd expect nothing less from someone working in the field known for paper-pushing. It's just the kind of nonsensical but impressive-sounding word to throw into the conversation when you want to go home early to stare into space. "If you'll excuse me, I've set the afternoon aside for epibreren." With a bit of luck your colleagues won't have a clue what you're talking about but, thinking they missed an important memo, they'll swallow it and let you go.

BULLSHIT LIST OF THINGS I'M SUPPOSED TO DO:
SHREDDER

NIKSEN AT WORK

For now, it's likely you need a job to put bread on the table, and that takes up a big chunk of your time. But that's not to say you can't do nothing at work. Those of you who think: *What, niksen at work? No way! We have to fire on all cylinders all day long.* Well, you're wrong. Work is the perfect place for a bit of slacking off, even if you're a fully booked heart surgeon or hairdresser, or a bus driver who can't step out from behind the wheel. It's virtually impossible to be "on" for eight hours straight. You can be physically present at work for that amount of time, but it's impossible to churn out one ingenious solution after another around the clock. You have to mix it up with a bit of guilt-free niksen. Your muscles need to recover from all that sitting or running around, and ideas need space to really come into their own. One little problem: You can't give yourself fully to doing nothing when you're watching the clock. When doing nothing, you don't want to feel pressed for time, because then it becomes just another item on your to-do list.

> Work is the perfect place for a bit of slacking off, even if you're a fully booked heart surgeon or hairdresser, or a bus driver who can't step out from behind the wheel.

Work is necessary for your personal humanity—it's surprising in a book about niksen, we know. Anyone who has ever been unemployed may be familiar with that empty feeling of not being needed. At the end of the day, we want to feel useful, whether it's in paid employment or elsewhere. In an ideal world, a work utopia suited to this day and age, labor would be tailored to each individual. That way, night owls don't have to clock in at 8:30 AM but can start at 10:00 or even later, just like students who get to decide when to study for exams and write their essays. Come to think of it, it's quite unnatural to spend the first twenty-odd years of life attending classes and deciding for yourself when and how you prove that you've grasped the course material, only to then find that for the next forty to fifty years you have to show up at fixed times to perform those skills. Instead, we can divide the day into smaller units. On average, people are most productive between 11:00 AM and 1:00 PM, so why not schedule all meetings and appointments in that window and do everything else in your own time? This may not benefit everyone, including shift workers (at least not yet), but with a change in office hours comes a change in mentality—and that's what we're after.

"What a way to make a living," sang Dolly Parton about the nine-to-five mentality. She's right. It's unnatural, especially when you're glued to an office chair all day, staring at small screens, attending back-to-back meetings. But we all know the robots are coming, and soon we'll be able to kick back and relax.

"What a way to make a living," sang Dolly Parton
about the nine-to-five mentality. She's right.
It's unnatural.

Not every boss is aware of the importance of naps, so they won't be thrilled when you turn up disheveled and with drool in the corner of your mouth. If your work environment isn't yet ready for The Big Sleep and flexible hours, you'll have to come up with some creative solutions to take breaks. You'll have to go underground, so to speak. Think of it this way: You're a member of a select club of pioneers/rebels/activists

Niksen with others is the ultimate good. Just lying in the grass, that sort of thing. I used to do it all the time, but as an adult everything is supposed to serve a purpose. What a revolting idea.

tom hofland*

* one of the Netherland's foremost literary talents

who understand that times change and that working so hard you hit a wall is no longer an option. The days of working until your head is about to explode with all the things you're trying to achieve are over. Sometimes, an escape is necessary.

One practical solution is the restroom. Perhaps not the most hygienic environment for your little act of resistance, but let's face it, every revolution demands small sacrifices. So how do you go about taking a nap in a restroom? Sit down in the cubicle with your clothes on, slumped. It would be good to have a beanie or a hoody to pull down over your eyes, so you can really disappear into dreamworld for a while. A tried and tested method, practiced by all the great minds, is holding a pen in your hand, so that when your body is completely relaxed you drop it and wake up. That way you'll avoid spending hours in the restroom and your colleagues won't send out a search party.

But what will people say? If that's a concern, you should a) stop worrying immediately, and b) just make a distressed face and no one will ask questions. Most people don't want to know why you just spent twenty-six minutes in the restroom.

One practical solution is the restroom. Perhaps not the most hygienic environment for your little act of resistance, but let's face it, every revolution demands small sacrifices.

Niksen at work also means not being "billable" all the time. This is the moment people start balking and say, "Wait, I'm a teacher; I can't leave a group of twenty students to their own devices. Before you know it they'll have stuck their hands together with super glue. I'm absolutely indispensable." If that's what you're thinking, then burnout is not far off. You're ready for sick leave. Everybody is dispensable—and that's how it should be, because otherwise the system will collapse any time a worker has a family emergency. Our whole system is based on non-load-bearing walls, and as soon as you think of yourself as a load-bearing wall, you need to take a break and get a sense of perspective. It's quite possible that you can't leave adolescents alone for five minutes, but you can occasionally let someone else deal with an issue. Get your house back in order—take care of yourself first, then others. In situations of compulsory attendance at work you can also make sure you're not doing extra work after hours. Don't spend your time for niksen in the evening answering emails with the aim of nipping future stress in the bud.

THE FUTURE

The Dutch journalist Wouter van Noort, in his reporting on the role of phones in our lives, wonders what we do with the extra time that should come with having handy apps and shortcuts. Of course, we spend that extra time on our phones. And no, three hours of aimless scrolling doesn't qualify as niksen.

How is it possible that we're spending so much time on our phones? As Wouter explains, "Much of the revenue of technological progress ends up in the pockets of big tech companies or in the market. These companies operate in an attention economy, in which data are the raw materials. This data is produced by us! We generate it with each online search and, given the way the system operates, we're effectively doing unpaid work for the Googles and Facebooks of this world. We've been turned into smartphone addicts, in part because these tech companies rely on us to generate all this data. . . . We think our lives have become easier, faster, and more frictionless, but in actual fact we're working really hard for the big tech players."

The online data economy looks to be free, because it doesn't cost consumers anything and it doesn't "bother" us. We can't even see it. Our phones let us send emails whenever we want and wherever we are, but they also feature games, news, and social media that take up hours of our day. As it turns out, "The idea that this technology is saving us time has proved to be completely false, because we spend big chunks of it on data production for companies that don't pay us a penny." Some have argued that if you're on Instagram two hours a day, the app really ought to pay you, because they can sell advertising based on your browsing behavior.

"According to Glen Weyl, the average person should perhaps be paid a thousand dollars a month by Google for all the work they do."

In 2016, Pokémon GO was released. The game tapped into our childhood nostalgia and generated a real buzz. So off we went to capture all these Pokémon, which had been scattered around the globe in the game's augmented reality. It's getting us out of the house! We're meeting people! It's amazing what a game can do. You could find a rare Pokémon on top of the Empire State Building and at the same time

meet the equally passionate love of your life. Later it emerged that Google was behind the app and that companies were paying the tech giant to get people into their shops. So there we were, thinking we were having fun by playing a game either alone or with a group of friends, when in actual fact we were being played.

Without realizing it, we're doing unpaid work, which is the exact opposite of niksen. Perhaps we should get paid for shopping! Wouter says, "Of course this eats into our time for doing nothing. The brain has two settings: On the one hand there's focus, and on the other niksen. When you're constantly distracted, those two settings become imbalanced. In a data economy, our attention becomes a commodity, and as a result we're unable to either fully focus or do nothing. It's a toxic cocktail. We now have a billion-dollar economy that revolves around distracting people and preventing them from concentrating. At the same time, the data economy is structured in such a way that we end up doing a lot of the work. A company like Amazon, for example, sends out lots of packages, and every time we accept one on behalf of a neighbor we effectively do the multinational's work. These companies hinge on outsourcing work to people who don't mind doing it for them."

The attention economy is booming. Companies are doing everything they can to capture our attention, even going as far as using methods derived from slot machines with catchy sounds and flashing lights. It's the same with media. They grab our attention with juicy headlines, according to Wouter. "Today, in the digital era, these age-old methods have been perfected to offer a more personalized service than ever. Companies have a pretty good idea who you are, especially when you haven't changed your privacy settings. It's terrifying to see how much they know about the dark side of your psyche—and that's exactly what they're targeting."

We now have a billion-dollar economy that revolves around distracting people and preventing them from concentrating.

What about the robots who are poised to take over our jobs, so we'll never have to work again and can dedicate ourselves to niksen? Wouter shatters that illusion and suggests that people routinely overestimate how happy new technologies will make them. The buzzword is *frictionless*—it's what the tech companies are targeting right now: Frictionless payments, for instance, so you can walk into a store and have your purchases automatically charged to your bank account via facial recognition technology. Amazon is already testing this technology in their stores. But when you take this utopia to extremes, when you go all the way and make everything frictionless, you end up with something you don't want. Wouter mentions the animated film *Wall-E*, which is all about robots, and has this scene of humans in spaceships: They move around in little automated cars while mindlessly gulping down milkshakes. They don't have to go to work; they have their own personalized entertainment systems and effectively spend the day doing nothing. All friction has been removed and lounging around maximized, but it hasn't made them any happier. As Frederick Douglass said, "Without friction, no polish." We always want something we don't have. Now that we have a fast-paced and efficient life full of innovative technology, we long to go back to a simpler life.

NIKSEN AROUND THE WORLD

Work has always been held in the highest regard in the Netherlands. It's even seen to shape a person's identity. That's why, when you meet new people, you're often asked, "So what do you do for a living?" Meanwhile, cultures all over the world are trying to find the ideal form of relaxation, not least because no one really knows why we're here on Earth. It's great that the planet has been around for 4.5 billion years and that humankind has been a part of it for several hundred thousand of those, but what is it all about? Are we the latest boy-toy of an aging Mother Earth, who has her family thinking: *OMG, he's going to bleed her dry and cheat us out of our inheritance! Are we a partner with a substance-abuse habit or borderline personality disorder?* That's what the other planets are thinking. It doesn't sound like a very honorable existence.

What's all this about, then? At the end of life, almost everyone agrees on one thing: It's definitely not about working till you drop. The consensus is that you have to make the best of it, and that means being nice to those around you, not killing anyone (which can be a challenge at times), and giving—and especially receiving—a lot of love. Being happy! It's a major theme in society. It's no small task—and we're constantly thwarted by other individuals who are equally eager to boost their own happiness. We're having to slow down, de-stress, and unfocus in order to chase a fleeting moment of happiness every day. All countries have found their own way of doing this. In the Netherlands, we hope niksen will fill that gap, but is there anything we can learn from other nations?

The French practice laissez-faire. Loosely translated as "to leave alone," the term is also used in economic theory to mean not interfering

in the market. For the average vacationer, however, it's more about letting things take their course. It sounds a bit callous: *If the house next door explodes, they can take care of it themselves, I'll just sit here with my magazines and madeleines.* Don't worry: It's not to be taken too literally; it's an expression, not a way of life.

Their days are punctuated only by breakfast, lunch, and dinner.

The Italians have *il dolce far niente*, "the sweetness of doing nothing"—and that's exactly what the Dutch niksen should aspire to. The Mediterranean sun clearly provides both warmth and wisdom. Of all the people in Europe, the Italians really know how to enjoy life. Niksen is a top priority in Italy. Or as the wonderfully named character Luca Spaghetti says to Liz Gilbert (played by Julia Roberts in her role as a stressed-out American in search of happiness) in the film *Eat Pray Love*:

> You feel guilty because you're American. You don't know how to enjoy yourself! Americans! You work too hard. You get burned out. Then you come home and spend the whole weekend in your pajamas in front of the TV. But you don't know pleasure. You have to be told you've earned it. But an Italian doesn't need to be told.

Fools that we Dutch are, for years we looked to the Americans with their big achievements and eighty-hour workweeks. We should have been watching more Italian films, which could have taught us a thing or two about il dolce far niente. Or else to American films set in Italy, like director Luca Guadagnino's *Call Me by Your Name*, which takes place during a seemingly never-ending summer in which the characters do sweet nothing all day, their days punctuated only by breakfast, lunch, and dinner.

MORE INSPIRATIONAL FILMS

1. ***The Big Lebowski*** (1998)
   This is an obvious one. The Dude (Jeff Bridges) saunters from the supermarket dairy aisle to the bowling alley. He's a freeloader who lives to be stoned. When he's mistaken for a millionaire called Lebowski he gets caught up in a kidnapping case (and a stolen rug). It's a terrific film about a man who has raised niksen to an art form.

2. ***Office Space*** (1999)
   Overworked Peter (Ron Livingston) is fed up with all the stupid rules at work and decides to start slacking off until he gets fired. His strategy is counterproductive, however, as he's promoted to an upper-management position. This film perfectly captures the reality of bullshit jobs.

3. ***Aanmodderfakker,*** or "How to Avoid Everything" (Dutch, 2014; available with English subtitles)
   An eternal student, Thijs has a boring job at a large electronics store but spends most of his time slacking off and successfully avoiding responsibility. When he takes his laundry to his sister, who is a mom and has her life together, he meets her incredibly attractive babysitter.

At the end of life, almost everyone agrees on one thing: It's definitely not about working till you drop.

The Spanish claim to be the champions of the siesta. The sad news is that the EU wanted Spain to abandon its traditional early-afternoon rest for economic reasons. It may also be because it has emerged that the Spanish were no longer using their siesta for a nap—but for a bit of niksen instead. After that, they would start on the second half of the day, and this ultimately resulted in nationwide sleep deprivation. Now that the Netherlands is warming up—and niksen will soon be common practice around the world—the time is ripe for us to have our own siesta debate. It's not that we should all chop our day in two with a big meal in the middle followed by rest, but we should at least have the option. It has long been argued that having the bulk of your daily food intake in the evening is not good for you. It's better to eat more at lunchtime and have a lighter meal in the evening.

In recent years, the Scandinavians have inundated the world with their lifestyle trends, including the quest for *lykke* (happiness), *hygge* (coziness), and *lagom* (literally "just the right amount," meaning being content with what you have). This is all wonderful, of course, but it has little to do with doing nothing. Remember: Niksen serves no purpose whatsoever. In his final book, *Island*, Aldous Huxley wrote about birds that had been trained to screech "Here and Now" while flying around the eponymous island. They were there to remind people to live in the present moment. Huxley knew it doesn't take much to get all worked up over work, a nasty remark made by the butcher, or the outcome of *The Great American Baking Show.* There's always something that doesn't sit well with you. The only Scandinavian trend that's related to the big adventure that is niksen is the Finnish concept of *pantsdrunk*: drinking beer (or something else) at home, alone, in your underwear. It comes pretty close. Except that you don't have to drink alcohol while doing nothing, and you can keep your clothes on, too. You don't have to, but you can. Half naked isn't always better.

On to the Brits. The United Kingdom has given us aristocratic idleness. Idleness isn't the same as laziness—it's more than that. Idleness also encompasses a sense that life is meaningless, which is a lot easier to live with when you're an aristocrat with enough time and money. Most people aren't in a position to take it easy and simply enjoy life, since they have a mortgage and other financial constraints. Only the aristocracy can afford to do nothing and come up with weird ways, such as cricket and polo, to pass the time.

The only Scandinavian trend that's related to the big adventure that is niksen is the Finnish concept of pantsdrunk: drinking beer (or something else) at home, alone, in your underwear.

FOREST BATHING in JAPAN

Let's skip a few countries and move on to Japan. The Japanese have various ways of chilling out. One of them is *shinrin-yoku*, or "forest bathing." The idea is to immerse yourself in nature, preferably a forest. Not literally, obviously, but by strolling through the forest and bathing in the atmosphere. It's imperative that while wandering around you use all five senses: sight, smell, hearing, touch, and taste. It has been shown to improve sleep, reduce stress, and boost your immune system. City dwellers, especially, have a habit of forgetting that there is such a thing as nature and that it's healthy to occasionally immerse yourself in it.

Japan is the gift that keeps on giving. It's also home to *chōwa*, a philosophy about the search for a balanced life. Anyone who's ever been to Japan knows that the place is seriously quiet. The streets of Tokyo are bustling, and yet you can hear someone clear their throat twenty feet away. And people form neat lines while they wait to board their train. It's a world away from the noisy chaos of the Netherlands—or America, for that matter. After a soccer match, or any other event, the Japanese clean up their mess. The Dutch think this is so extraordinary that it merits a news report every time it happens. The Japanese do *what* now? Grab a shopping bag and pick up their litter?! What's happening is an example of chōwa: balance. Keeping everything clutter-free and not wanting too many earthly possessions is vital to maintaining a healthy balance. That same balance can be achieved via recycling by repurposing material you've already used with gratitude, both in your home and elsewhere.

Here's one such news item, from *Jeugdjournaal*, a Dutch news program aimed at children: "It was a lovely gesture from the players of Japan's national soccer team. Yesterday they lost 3–2 to Belgium thanks to a last-minute goal. Though a huge disappointment, it didn't stop them from cleaning everything up afterward." They lost the match, but left the place as they found it. The Dutch would never do that, especially not after a defeat. Just be glad there's no casual vandalism.

Japan is the gift that keeps on giving.
It's also home to *chōwa*, a philosophy about the search for a balanced life.

And if that wasn't enough, the Japanese also give us *ikigai*. This practice is about finding a purpose in life, something that makes life worth living, an endless source of joy—so endless you don't want to retire. The Japanese have a habit of living to a ripe old age, so it's clearly working! You can determine this purpose with the help of a kind of Venn diagram involving four circles that represent what you love, what you're good at, what the world needs, and what you can be paid for. Where four circles overlap, that's where your ikigai is.

Ikigai is about searching for and finding happiness. It's a beautiful thing to strive for, but again, it's not niksen because it serves a purpose. Once you've finally found your niche, a place where you totally belong and feel completely at home, and when you're in touch with your emotions, there will still be moments when you don't feel all that great—at those times you may need to complement ikigai with niksen.

It sounds like anyone who wants to find inner calm should simply move to Japan. Japan seems to have it all: peace and quiet, a booming economy, great design, and the art of finding balance while forest bathing—not to mention ikigai, an appreciation for the beauty of imperfection (*wabi-sabi*), sushi, and sky-high life expectancy. There's certainly a lot we can learn from the Japanese, but when you move to another country, you don't copy and paste only the best bits of a culture. If you moved to Japan, chances are you'd discover they're really

UKIYO

[u-key-yo] • JAPANESE •

(n) living in the moment, detached from every day worries

[literally: the floating world]

bad at some things, too, like talking about their emotions. And they're not very sympathetic when you break a law you didn't even know existed. The Dutch have a popular TV series called *I'm Off*, which features Dutch people trying their luck abroad and shows plenty of examples of this. Besides, wherever you go, you always take yourself with you. We'd better practice *kaizen*—the Japanese method of taking small steps to big change—and continuously adapt and improve.

> But when you move to another country, you don't copy and paste only the best bits of a culture. If you moved to Japan, chances are you'd discover they're really bad at some things, too, like talking about their emotions.

We could have cited all of Buddhism in this section, as it's full of reasons for doing nothing and letting go of things that trouble you. Take, for example, the concept of "don't-know mind," which is said to originate in Korea. One of the people to write about this is Zen Master Seung Sahn, the former teacher of mindfulness guru Jon Kabat-Zinn. Don't-know mind involves forgetting everything you know, including awareness of your surroundings, words, and the self, in order to be one with the universe. This is incredibly difficult, next-level stuff, and impossible for an untrained mind. Seung Sahn observes, "Thinking is desire and desire is suffering." He even counters Descartes's famous motto, "I think therefore I am," by asking: "What if you're not thinking—then what?" He likens thought to a prison. "In each moment, just let go of your opinion, condition, and situation. Then you become clear. When you are doing something, just do it. This is everyday Zen." Even if you don't have the time or the inclination to plunge deeply into Zen Buddhism, you can still work with the don't-know idea. Just tell yourself you don't know.

Imagine you're on a train, sitting opposite someone who's getting all dolled up, using all kinds of strong-smelling products like hairspray and nail polish. You have a choice: You can become all agitated and think, *Can't you do that at home?!* That's a perfectly logical but totally un-Zen reaction. *Un-Zen!* You could also think to yourself: *I don't know. Maybe this person is on their way to a super-important job interview that their future depends on, but they live in a house with sixteen others and none of the bathrooms were free, or something along these lines.* How might this help you with niksen? By professing not to know, you can rid yourself of quite a few irritations; sit down, relax, and stare into space instead.

All over the world people are trying to enjoy life more, and we can learn from their approaches. Obviously, no country is populated entirely by slackers—the pressure to make something of our lives is simply too great—but there are plenty of ways to enjoy the finer things just a bit more.

> At fifteen I set my mind on learning; by thirty I had found my footing; at forty I was free of perplexities; by fifty I understood the will of Heaven; by sixty I learned to give ear to others; by seventy I could follow my heart's desires without overstepping the line.

Does this sound like a contemporary self-help mantra? These words are actually from Confucius, who lived around the fifth century BCE.

CREATIVITY

In recent years, living life to the fullest has become a hot topic. We've even built an entire happiness industry around it, which is all about meeting targets. And that's the problem: yet more goals to strive for. Use your brain in a smarter, better, faster way! Become happier! "Live your best life" is a catchy slogan, but it also creates more pressure. It has undertones that suggest: Unless your life is extraordinary and exciting it's not worth much. No wonder you feel guilty when you're watching old episodes of *Friends* over and over again. You're not making the best use of your time. On top of it all, you're living in the land of plenty that people in the Middle Ages dreamed of, just so they wouldn't have to think about hunger and pestilence. We have enough to eat (around the clock), no longer have to toil for eighty hours a week in the freezing cold, and

we have apps for sex. Perhaps the answer to the question "Why is it so hard to be like a cat and do nothing but sleep for hours on end?" lies in our society, in the world around us.

When our head is clear and we walk out the door whistling, other people bother us with their to-do lists. We can't spend a single moment doing nothing without being made to feel guilty. You don't need a reason to goof off for half an hour or longer every day. The point is to let go of all those stress-inducing, modern-day urges to improve ourselves. Niksen doesn't have to lead anywhere. Obviously, you can't solve a massive problem by not thinking about it, though many have tried. It's called compartmentalization, and if you have a habit of doing this, you'll end up needing therapy because your body will hold on to too many unresolved issues. Since society is not yet completely ready to embrace aimless niksen, we'll set out a few additional benefits. Hopefully, these will motivate you to do nothing every once in a while.

A creative person, however brilliant, isn't a genius 24-7.

Not stepping in but just letting things just take their course can work out amazingly well sometimes. Like everything in life, creativity is all about finding the right balance. While you're doing nothing, the most brilliant ideas can suddenly pop into your head. J. K. Rowling came up with the idea for Harry Potter on a crowded train. She freaked out because she didn't have pen and paper with her, but the journey gave her hours to just sit and let her imagination run wild about the school where students with special gifts are taught seven unusual subjects.

Niksen may give creatives a boost, but it can also give them a bad name. Artists often have the dubious reputation of being freeloaders who can only get by with help from rich donors or government grants, to do nothing is the most difficult thing in the world... the most difficult and the most intellectual.

oscar wilde

whose largesse forces them to get off their lazy asses once a month to paint a line on some surface and call it *One Line, No Cross*, or *Untitled 243545*. Real artistry is hard work, though. First of all, dealing with this kind of prejudice can be tough. And then there's the vague way in which creativity comes about. A creative person, however brilliant, isn't a genius 24-7. They also have moments of stupidity when they can't think of the name of their least favorite uncle, not to mention those times when they think: *Am I good enough?*

No wonder you feel guilty when you're watching
old episodes of *Friends* over and over again.
You're not making the best use of your time.

Three years after her mega bestseller *Eat, Pray, Love*, Elizabeth Gilbert delivered a TED Talk about the pressure she felt in response to people's expectations. She'd get asked questions like, "Aren't you afraid you're never going to be able to top that?"—in effect, that she'd be consumed by self-hatred and end up in the gutter, choking on her own vomit. She acknowledged the fear and attributed the problem to the artist's ego. Until the Renaissance it was thought that artists had what the Greeks described as a "divine attendant spirit" and the Romans a "genius," Gilbert explained. It was a kind of magical force that brought them to their creations, both good and bad. Neither the success nor the failure was something they could take sole credit for, because the work didn't originate with them. This all changed during the Renaissance, when individualism was in vogue, the idea of the divine spirit was abandoned, and the artist/scientist was suddenly proclaimed a genius. This belief puts too much pressure on creatives, Gilbert thinks, and we should reintroduce the idea of an external power.

"You don't want to get tense—you just kind of play with the thought. And then little ideas start popping up." The beauty of niksen in a nutshell.

Monty Python icon John Cleese has read, written, and spoken extensively about creativity and where in god's name it comes from. In 2014, when he was interviewed on the Dutch TV show *College Tour*, he attributes it to one's mental state: "It all boils down to getting into a playful and relaxed frame of mind. Most of it's to do with relaxation. Because unless you're relaxed you can't hear the promptings from the unconscious." This unconscious sounds similar to the "genius" cited by Gilbert. Cleese believes there's so little creativity at the moment because "nobody gets any peace anymore." People are distracted all day, with their minds pulled into a million different directions. Thanks to the internet, we can be in a thousand places at once: on a date in a café having wine and cheese, while at the same time messaging a friend in crisis and your father who is worried about his impending retirement. As Cleese says, "Interruptions and anxiety will kill any kind of creativity." What you want is

> a little cocoon of your own. You close your door, or you go and sit in the park and just stay quiet. And for twenty minutes nothing happens, because you can only think of the things you ought to be doing or the people you've forgotten to telephone, so you have to have a little notebook and you write those down. And after twenty minutes the mind starts to calm down, just as it does in meditation—it's an almost identical process. And then, when you start thinking about the subject—not too hard, you don't want to get tense—you just kind of play with the thought. And then you get little ideas starting to pop up.

The beauty of niksen in a nutshell.

Creativity can't be summoned at will, but it's possible to set aside a moment for yourself when you try to let go of everything, allow your mind to wander, and jot down ideas or items for your to-do list for the practical part of your day.

NIKSERS OF NOTE

Ambling about (or as the Dutch say: *aankutten*, another one of those untranslatable words) can lead to creativity. Neurologists say so, and even artists believe it. For the list lovers among you, here's a selection of niksers of note!

- Salvador Dalí: perfected the art of napping
- Leonardo da Vinci: advised against working too hard
- Federico Fellini: a fan of slacking off
- Gustav Mahler: loved going for long walks
- Gertrude Stein: liked to look at cows when taking breaks from her writing
- Dolly Parton: "Don't get so busy making a living that you forget to make a life." A great Dollyism for a happy life!

INSPIRATION

Sometimes you run out of inspiration and can't decide what to make for dinner, or what new Instagram account to launch. You're stumped for ideas, and you think, *What's trendy?* Perhaps that will get you started. Nope, nothing sparks inspiration. So you think: *Pfff, never mind. I'm going to take a shower.* And then, *bam*, there it is: pasta alla puttanesca, that surprising combination of anchovies, olives, and capers in a warm bath of pureed tomatoes. *That's it!* Despite what it may seem like, this new inspiration isn't a question of *presto* and up it pops—it's been simmering in your mind for weeks. And when you take it easy for a moment, your brain suddenly makes a crazy connection, one that may not seem logical at first, but that turns out to make perfect sense. It takes a lot of time, but also a lot of rest.

UNFOCUSING

The psychiatrist Srini Pillay, MD, is a fierce proponent of slacking off during the day. There's no point in racking your brain from morning till night; at times you have to unfocus. In his book *Tinker Dabble Doodle Try: Unlock the Power of the Unfocused Mind*, he writes that people generally don't jump for joy when he tells them to unfocus more. "They think it means they should relax their standards or flit around aimlessly. They don't want to become (or continue to be) dilettantes; they want to be producers and problem solvers. The mention of tinkering, dabbling, doodling, and trying elicits a similar reaction." In the Netherlands people are suspicious of the jack-of-all-trades who starts but never finishes projects. But being unfocused is good for you. Dr. Pillay agrees. He lists several forms of unfocusing, like reverie (talking about your thoughts as they arise), daydreaming, and self-talk (talking to yourself in your mind). These activities are—you've guessed it—typical of niksen.

There's no point in racking your brain from morning till night; at times you have to unfocus.

Dr. Pillay also writes extensively about the brain's default mode network (DMN), the part that's (quite) active when you're doing nothing. Scientists long thought that not much happened in these areas of the brain, but research has shown just how important it is, especially in relation to mental illness and diseases such as Alzheimer's. It's important to our ability to draw connections and be creative. You can strengthen your DMN by training it every once in a while—for instance, by picking two items in a room and trying to link them, or by doodling.

PROCRASTINATION

The time you spend not doing the work you really should be doing lends itself extremely well to doing nothing. Putting things off is one of humanity's perennial "problems." You may have a presentation due tomorrow morning, and suddenly time becomes elastic. It occurs to you that you used to be really creative at night, way back in high school. Or you figure you could set the alarm for 4:00 AM, which would give you five whole hours to finish your presentation. This is procrastination. Can we deploy it without hating ourselves for it?

Procrastination has been around for centuries. While it's often seen as a bad habit of lazy people, procrastination can also be a sign that you're not quite ready to do something. Perhaps you can't wait to check an item off of your to-do list but still find yourself putting off the most important tasks. The British actress Jennifer Saunders swears by procrastination. She says she needs it for her creativity. Instead of buckling down on writing her screenplay, she chooses to work in the garden, cultivating all of her ideas before cutting back the bad ones. Then again, these delaying tactics could also be a lame excuse for why the script wasn't finished until the eleventh hour. It's understandable that you condemn yourself for procrastinating, especially when facing a deadline. The story goes that Victor Hugo had his formal clothes locked away so he would have no choice but to stay at home all day and write, wrapped in a large woolen shawl, until he'd finished his book.

Gustave Flaubert hit a wall while writing *Madame Bovary*. He said:

> Sometimes, when I am empty, when words don't come, when I find I haven't written a single sentence after scribbling whole pages, I collapse on my couch and lie there dazed, bogged down in a swamp of despair, hating myself and blaming myself for this demented pride that makes me pant after a chimera. A quarter of an hour later, everything has changed; my heart is pounding with joy.

See, that's the amazing effect of niksen right there. All those awful thoughts about yourself, the anguish, the fear of failure—they need an outlet.

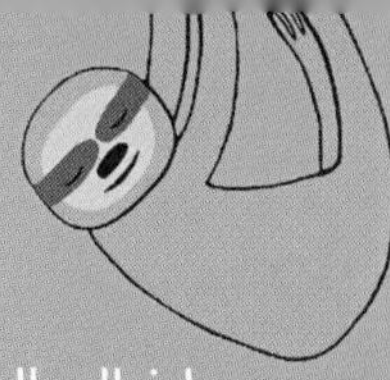

FREELOADERS

Of all the layabouts in the literary world, the character Ilya Ilyich Oblomov is perhaps the most famous. The mid-nineteenth-century author Ivan Goncharov wrote the novel *Oblomov*, and it's not that his titular character doesn't want to do anything, he just can't get out of bed. On the rare occasions when he manages to get up, life doesn't agree with him and he goes back to bed. The question is: Is he lazy or depressed? If the former, he can't count on much sympathy from us; we tend to think that slackers need a kick in the backside and not much else. If the latter, Oblomov may be in better luck. We're beginning to have more understanding for people with depression, as we recognize that not everyone has the resilience to deal with life's daunting questions (like: What's life all about?).

There's a fine line between niksen and laziness, as the Dutch author Nescio showed in his short story "The Freeloader," featuring Japi, a man who aspires to be a bohemian. The name comes from the Romany of Bohemia, a region in what is now the Czech Republic, and was adopted by several French sophisticates in the nineteenth century keen to live the laissez-faire lifestyle. Japi lives by the grace of other people: by what they discard as well as the kindness of their hearts. He isn't just into taking it easy, he's more hard-core than that. He wants to, as he says, "overcome the body." While a freeloader, Japi's one wish is

> To no longer feel hunger or exhaustion, cold, or rain. Those were the great enemies. You always had to eat and sleep, over and over again, you had to get out of the cold, you got wet and tired or miserable. Now look at that water. It has it good: it just ripples and reflects the clouds, it's always changing and yet always stays the same, too. Has no problems at all.

Unfortunately, though Japi isn't lazy, he can't overcome his body by freeloading. He's forced to go to work, forfeiting niksen, and that proves to be his undoing.

PRACTICAL TIPS:

Fighting distraction

When your head's full of stuff you'd rather not think about, and you feel as though you're going insane or you're on the verge of burnout, you may fall victim to distraction. Here are some tips to get you back on track.

Switch off your smartphone.

We're living in an age in which multitasking has become the norm, with smartphones as a source of endless distraction. We're still going through work emails over dinner, reading the news, and second-guessing every decision we made throughout the day. This is more likely in some professions than others, but anyone can receive negative feedback in their inbox and accidentally look at it in the evening or on vacation. Constantly being on email generates fresh input for your churning mind and ruins your niksen. Try switching the device to airplane mode while doing nothing.

Adopt a guinea pig.

Or a cat—any cute and cuddly nocturnal creature will do. As long as it's a quiet animal that either spends much of the day zonked out or lives by night and sleeps during the day, and that's fascinating to watch. A guinea pig is absolutely perfect. Make sure it sleeps somewhere far from your bed so it doesn't keep you awake at night. Technically speaking, cuddling a guinea pig doesn't qualify as doing nothing—you're cuddling a guinea pig, that's to say, you're paying attention to another living being. But it can be a useful tool for calming yourself down if you can't find peace and quiet any other way. Just don't forget: A guinea pig or any other pet needs looking after. Some might ask whether it's selfish to adopt an animal purely for your own pleasure. Um . . . why else adopt a pet? Give us a good reason that isn't 100 percent selfish. Saving an animal from a shelter, perhaps, but even then you're putting your own interests first. We have yet to meet someone who didn't really want a guinea pig but who felt so sorry for it that they decided to sacrifice their own happiness just to give the creature a better life. That's another debate. For now, let's stick to doing nothing.

Do nothing in a place where you like to be.

As mentioned, you need to create space in your head for niksen. Likewise, it helps to create a place—or a little corner in your house—that you're proud of. Perhaps you once put up your own bookshelf, or you have a plant that's still alive three years after you bought it. These provide positive conditions for doing nothing. You can watch them and compliment yourself on your success. Or if someone else put up the shelf, be thankful. With this excellent foundation in place, you can retreat into a lovely dreamworld.

Save it for a rainy day.

Make sure all your basic needs have been met: You've been to the bathroom, you've eaten or have nice food in the house for later, and above all you're not wearing uncomfortable clothing. Niksen while wearing a belt that's cutting into your stomach isn't much fun. And doing nothing is done best in a place where the temperature is just right: not too hot, not too cold. If you're really hopeless at doing nothing, try starting on a rainy day. It won't feel so weird that instead of going out to buy supplies to finally fix up your roof terrace, you're just sitting on the couch, watching the rain.

CONCLUSION

By now, we hope we're all on the same page, and that page, says: Take it easy. Our lives are like a carnival ride spinning out of control, and—dizzy from our turn on the carousel—we're in need of cotton candy to get our blood sugar level back to normal. For centuries, we've been working toward a life in which we can relax and enjoy all of our achievements. Even the earth itself could do with a less frenetic pace right now.

We're ready to become the people who love doing glorious nothing. It's time to go from the disapproving "Stop being a lazy so-and-so" to the encouraging "Oh nice, you're doing nothing!"

We're living the medieval dream and it's only getting better. Slowly but surely the way we work is changing, and with all the technology at our disposal we don't even have to leave the house anymore, for anything. If we do want to go outside—for some fresh air, perhaps—all of our interactions can be "frictionless." In outlining this scenario we're assuming that the world's leaders will stay out of one another's hair and that none of them have evil intentions. You never know what the future holds, and so we'd better learn to make the most of the present—and learn to do absolutely nothing.

During our research, and the interviews and conversations we had with each other and with experts, we often wondered: How is it possible that we still can't seem to slow down a bit? Why do we keep thinking that our world has to be better, faster, and smarter?

We're ready to become the people who love doing glorious nothing! It's time to go from the disapproving "Stop being a lazy so-and-so" to the encouraging "Oh nice, you're doing nothing!" In a perfect world, when walking by a group of people hanging out, another passerby will comment, "Oh, good for them, they're doing nothing." It will be the same way that we tiptoe past the dog when she's lying in her basket and drooling.

And now you can toss this book aside, and finally stare out of the window for a while.

FURTHER READING

Eyal, Nir. *Indistractable: How to Control Your Attention and Choose Your Life*. Benbella Books, 2019.

Gini, Al. *The Importance of Being Lazy: In Praise of Play, Leisure, and Vacation*. Routledge, 2003.

Postman, Neil. *Amusing Ourselves to Death: Public Discourse in the Age of Show Business*. Penguin, 2005.

Lightman, Alan. *In Praise of Wasting Time*. Simon & Schuster, 2018.

Maas, Angela. *A Woman's Heart: Why Female Heart Health Really Matters*. Hachette, 2020.

Toohey, Peter. *Boredom: A Lively History*. Yale University Press, 2012.

Thoreau, Henry David. *Walden; or, Life in the Woods*. Ticknor and Fields, 1854; Signet, 2012.

Pleij, Herman. *Dreaming of Cockaigne: Medieval Fantasies of the Perfect Life*. Translated by Diane Webb. Columbia University Press, 2003.

ABOUT THE AUTHORS

MAARTJE WILLEMS is a Dutch journalist and writer. She lives in Amsterdam where she works as a freelancer and for the VPRO radio program *Never Sleep Again*. She previously wrote the self-help book *Vanaf nu wordt alles beter* (From now on everything will get better).

MaartjeWillems.nl

LONA AALDERS is a photographer and illustrator. She lives in a tiny house in Baambrugge and sees slow living as her personal religion. She previously authored the book *Bullet journaling: zo doe je dat* (Bullet journaling: this is how you do it!) and illustrated *Vanaf nu wordt alles beter* for Maartje Willems.

Lona-Aalders.com